managing your personal finances with quicken

Visual QuickProject Guide

by Tom Negrino

Peachpit Press

Visual QuickProject Guide
Managing Your Personal Finances with Quicken
Tom Negrino

Peachpit Press
1249 Eighth Street
Berkeley, CA 94710
510/524-2178
800/283-9444
510/524-2221 (fax)

Find us on the World Wide Web at: www.peachpit.com
To report errors, please send a note to errata@peachpit.com
Peachpit Press is a division of Pearson Education

Copyright © 2005 by Tom Negrino

Editor: Nancy Davis
Production Editor: Connie Jeung-Mills
Compositor: Owen Wolfson
Indexer: Rebecca Plunkett
Cover design: The Visual Group with Aren Howell
Interior design: Elizabeth Castro
Cover photo credit: Photodisc

SUFFOLK COUNTY COUNCIL	
06399137	
Cypher	04.02.05
332.024	£9.99
531194	

Notice of Rights
All rights reserved. No part of this book may be reproduced or transmitted in any form by any means, electronic, mechanical, photocopying, recording, or otherwise, without the prior written permission of the publisher. For information on getting permission for reprints and excerpts, contact permissions@peachpit.com.

Notice of Liability
The information in this book is distributed on an "As Is" basis, without warranty. While every precaution has been taken in the preparation of the book, neither the author nor Peachpit Press shall have any liability to any person or entity with respect to any loss or damage caused or alleged to be caused directly or indirectly by the instructions contained in this book or by the computer software and hardware products described in it.

Trademarks
Visual QuickProject Guide is a registered trademark of Peachpit Press, a division of Pearson Education.
All other trademarks are the property of their respective owners.

Throughout this book, trademarks are used. Rather than put a trademark symbol with every occurrence of a trademarked name, we state that we are using the names in an editorial fashion only and to the benefit of the trademark owner with no intention of infringement of the trademark. No such use, or the use of any trade name, is intended to convey endorsement or other affiliation with this book.

ISBN 0-321-29365-7

9 8 7 6 5 4 3 2 1

Printed and bound in the United States of America

To my father, Joe Negrino, who has led his accounting clients through the thorny underbrush of the tax system for half a century.

Special Thanks to...

My superb editor, Nancy Davis.

The book's production editor, Connie Jeung-Mills.

Aruna Harder and Chris Repetto of Intuit, for their help with questions about Quicken 2005 for Windows and Macintosh.

This Book Is Safari Enabled

The Safari® Enabled icon on the cover of your favorite technology book means the book is available through Safari Bookshelf. When you buy this book, you get free access to the online edition for 45 days.

Safari Bookshelf is an electronic reference library that lets you easily search thousands of technical books, find code samples, download chapters, and access technical information whenever and wherever you need it.

To gain 45-day Safari Enabled access to this book:

- Go to http://www.peachpit.com/safarienabled
- Complete the brief registration form
- Enter the coupon code 09KB-TXYJ-NKJW-W4J5-Y3UQ

If you have difficulty registering on Safari Bookshelf or accessing the online edition, please e-mail customer-service@safaribooksonline.com.

contents

1. explore quicken — 1

create data file (Win)	2	quicken for mac	9
create data file (Mac)	4	explore toolbars	12
quicken for windows	5	extra bits	15

2. set up your finances — 17

decide what to manage	18	set up categories (Win)	25
set up accounts (Win)	19	set up categories (Mac)	27
set up accounts (Mac)	22	extra bits	28
about categories	24		

3. set up your paycheck — 31

paycheck setup (Win)	32	extra bits	40
paycheck setup (Mac)	36		

4. write and print checks — 41

explore registers	42	transfer money	52
enter transactions	43	write checks	54
split transactions	45	print checks	56
edit transactions	47	extra bits	57
schedule transactions	48		

5. bank and pay bills online — 61

set up online accounts	62	use one step update	75
use Web Connect	66	create online payees	77
compare transactions	68	pay bills online	79
organize your pins (Win)	73	transfer money online	80
organize your pins (Mac)	74	extra bits	82

v

contents

6. balance your accounts — 85

balance accounts	86	extra bits	91
correct differences	89		

7. manage your credit cards and mortgage — 93

enter card charges	94	make loan payments	102
make card payments	95	track your mortgage	104
mortgage setup (Win)	96	extra bits	105
mortgage setup (Mac)	99		

8. create reports and graphs — 107

get EasyAnswers	108	create graphs	115
use standard reports	110	print reports or graphs	117
build custom reports	111	extra bits	118
save custom reports	113		

9. set up and track investments — 119

how much detail?	120	view security details	129
portfolio setup (Win)	121	download quotes	131
portfolio setup (Mac)	125	extra bits	132
use portfolio window	127		

10. manage investments — 133

add transactions (Win)	134	deal with dividends	138
add transactions (Mac)	136	extra bits	140

index — 141

introduction

The Visual QuickProject Guide that you hold in your hands offers a unique way to learn about new technologies. Instead of drowning you in theoretical possibilities and lengthy explanations, this Visual QuickProject Guide uses big, color illustrations coupled with clear, concise step-by-step instructions to show you how to complete one specific project in a matter of hours.

Our project in this book is to gain control of your personal finances using the latest version of the best-selling personal finance program, Quicken. You can use either Quicken 2005 for Windows or Quicken 2005 for Macintosh. These are the latest versions, but if you haven't upgraded yet, don't fret; because Quicken doesn't change too much from year to year, things will look pretty familiar if you have earlier versions.

I'll show you how to use Quicken to handle your paycheck; manage your checkbook; bank and pay bills online; balance your accounts to the penny every month; manage your credit cards; and handle your investments.

what you'll create

Create a data file in Quicken to contain all of your financial information.

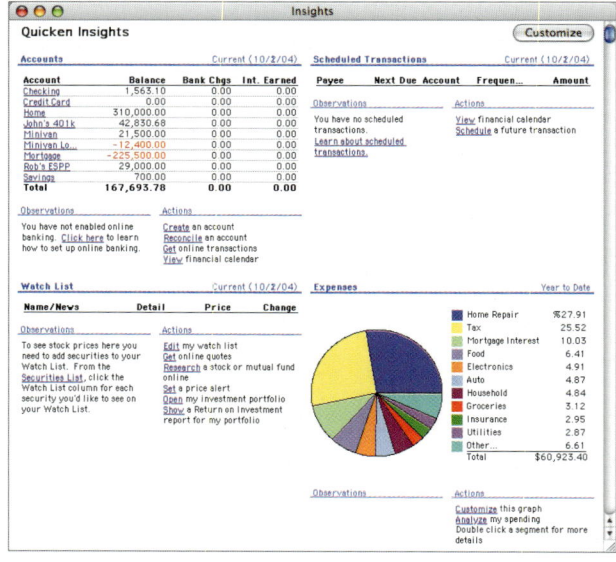

Create accounts in Quicken that correspond to your checking, savings, credit card, and investment accounts in the real world, and see at a glance your account balances.

Set up your paycheck and schedule it so that Quicken automatically enters the paycheck information every time you get paid.

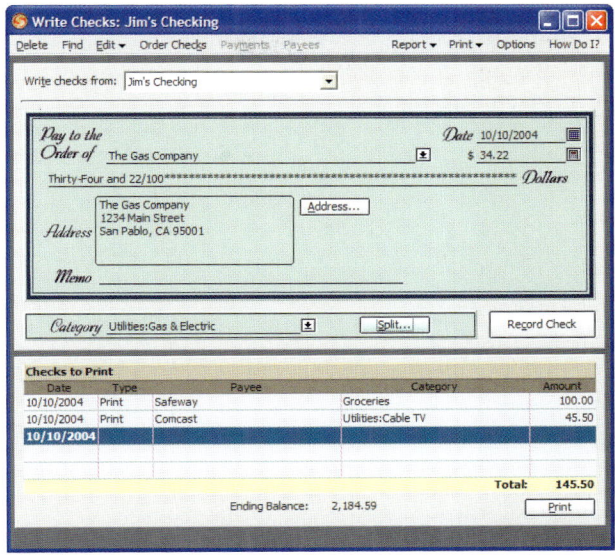

You'll learn how to write checks in Quicken, and, if you like, print checks from the program on pre-printed check forms.

Never forget a bill again—just put regular bills into Quicken and tell it to memorize the bill. Quicken reminds you to pay the bill every month, banishing late fees forever!

Tired of writing checks? You can pay your bills from within Quicken with online banking and online bill payment. This saves you time and effort, and as a bonus, it takes literally seconds each month to reconcile your checkbook.

Credit cards are great, but they can be cruel masters if you let your spending get out of hand. You'll learn to use Quicken to keep on top of credit card debt and prevent it from spiraling out of control.

Quicken's reports and graphs are great tools to let you know where your finances stand. You'll see how to use them for a quick financial checkup.

Looking forward to retirement? Smart investing now will pay off in the years ahead. You'll see how to set up your investment accounts, and how you can keep on top of your portfolio as it grows in value.

how this book works

The title of each section explains what is covered on that page.

Important terms and Web site addresses are shown in orange.

Captions explain what you're doing and why. They also point to items of interest.

Numbered steps explain actions to perform in a specific order.

add transactions (Win)

1 Choose Buy – Shares Bought from the investment transactions pop-up menu.

2 Enter the Transaction date.

3 Choose the security you want to purchase from the Security name pop-up menu. This menu lists all the securities you have previously bought. If you are buying a security that is new to your portfolio, click the Add New Security button at the bottom of the pop-up menu, and Quicken will walk you through a quick Wizard to add the new security.

Add New Security

4 Enter the number of shares you have bought in the Number of shares field.

5 Enter the price you paid per share in the Price paid field.

6 If you paid a broker commission, enter its dollar amount in the Commission field. Quicken calculates the cost of the transaction (number of shares times price per share plus commission) and places the result in the Total cost field.

7 If you want to add a memo, type it in the Memo field.

8 The money to pay for your purchase can either come from the cash balance in your portfolio account or from another Quicken account, such as your checking account. If it comes from the portfolio cash balance, in the Use cash for this transaction section, click From this account's cash balance. If the money comes from another account, click From, and then choose the account from the pop-up menu next to it.

9 If you want to save the current transaction and immediately enter another, click Enter/New. If you are done entering transactions, click Enter/Done. The investment transaction is saved, and it appears in the Transactions tab of the investment account.

manage investments   **135**

x   **introduction**

The extra bits section at the end of each chapter contains additional tips and tricks that you might like to know—but that aren't absolutely necessary for creating the presentation.

The heading for each group of tips matches the section title.

The page number next to the heading makes it easy to refer back to the main content.

introduction

useful tools

Quicken is pretty self-contained in terms of managing your finances, but there are lots of useful sites on the Web that can help you manage your money.

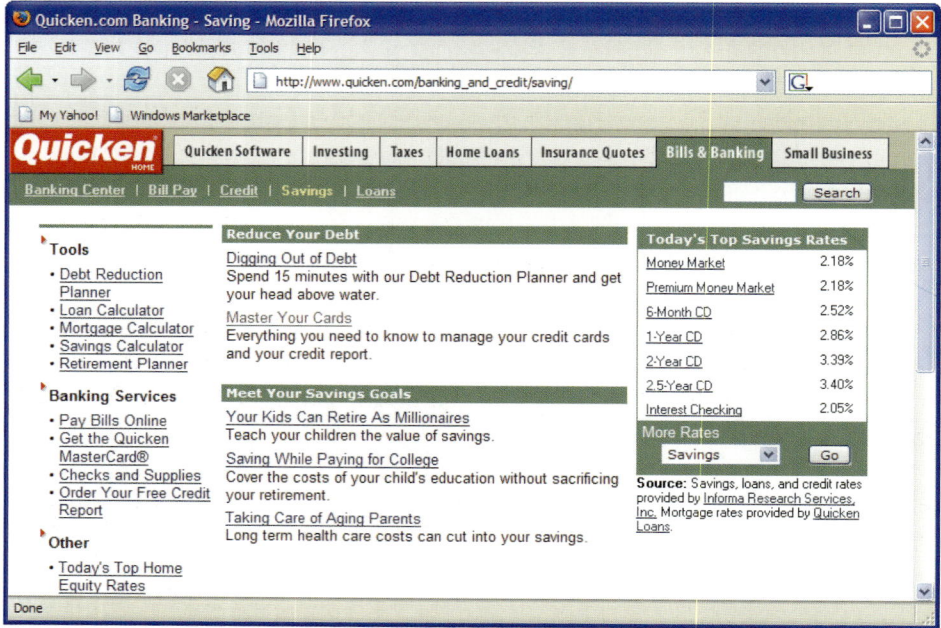

To view these sites, you'll need an Internet connection (a broadband connection is best) and a Web browser. On Windows, you'll probably use Internet Explorer, and on the Mac, Apple's Safari. If you're a Windows user, I suggest using Mozilla Firefox as your Web browser (shown); it's much less susceptible to viruses and other bad software than is Internet Explorer for Windows. When you're talking about your money, the more security, the better. You can obtain Firefox at http://www.mozilla.org.

1. explore quicken

Before you start working with Quicken, you need to see the tools that Quicken gives you. In this chapter, you'll explore the user interface from two versions of Quicken: Quicken 2005 for Windows and Quicken 2005 for Macintosh. Though the two programs look different, both deliver all of the financial savvy you need to manage your money.

On Windows, there are four versions of Quicken 2005, with increasing amounts of features and capabilities: Basic, Deluxe, Premier, and Premier Home & Business. On the Macintosh, there's just one version, called Quicken 2005 for Mac.

Start up Quicken. On Windows, point at the Start menu, choose Programs, then choose Quicken, and then choose Quicken 2005.

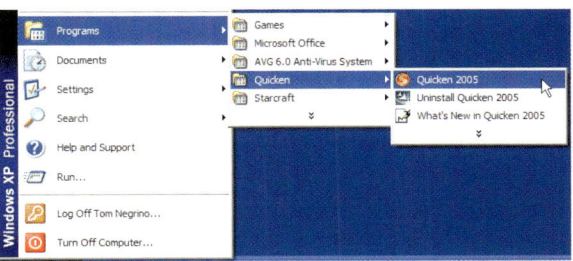

On the Mac, open the Applications folder, then open the Quicken 2005 folder, and double-click on the Quicken 2005 icon.

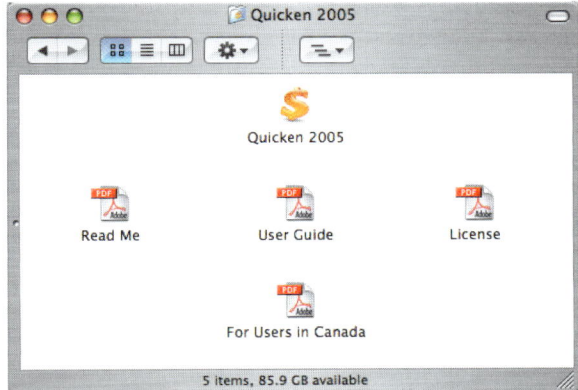

create data file (Win)

When you start up Quicken for the first time on Windows, it launches the Get Started Assistant.

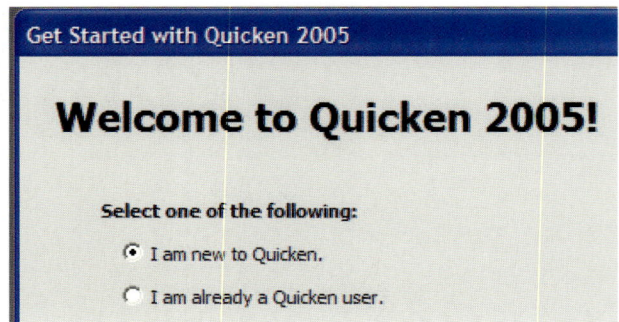

Choose I am new to Quicken and click Next. In the next screen, Quicken asks you what you want to call your data file. By default, the name is QDATA and will end up in your My Documents folder. That's a fine location, but the name isn't very helpful, so select I want to choose a different file name and location and click Next.

In the resulting Create Quicken File dialog, give the file a descriptive name (I suggest your last name) and click OK. In this book, we'll be following the financial adventures of the fictional Carroll family, so I named the file Carroll Family.

When the file is created, Quicken Guided Setup starts up automatically. This is another assistant in which you enter a bunch of information, and it tries to set up your accounts for you. I think it's overkill, so we'll enter data on just one of the Guided Setup screens, then strike out on our own. The first screen is just informational, so read it and click Next Step.

On the About You screen, enter all the information requested, including your name and birthdate (Quicken uses your birthdate for retirement calculations); if you're married, enter your spouse's information. Then click Exit Setup. Quicken saves what you entered.

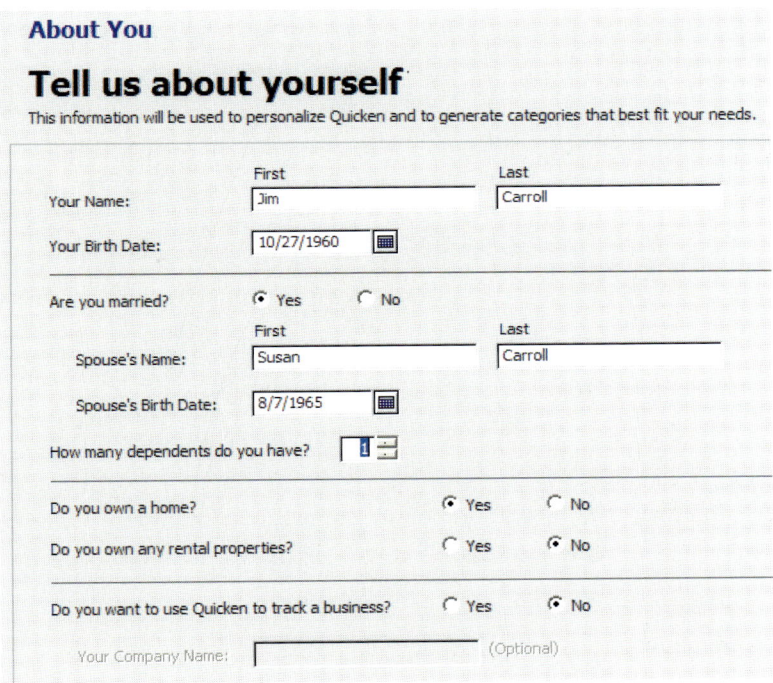

explore quicken

create data file (Mac)

On the Mac, Quicken displays an Open dialog, asking for the location of your data file (it assumes that you are upgrading from a previous version). Click Cancel, then choose File > New File. In the resulting Save dialog, give the data file a descriptive name (something more interesting than Quicken Data, such as Carroll Family), and choose where you want to save it. Quicken comes with a set of categories that will help you organize your finances. You'll learn more about categories in Chapter 2; for now, if you'll be using Quicken for your home finances, just select the Home check box, and if you also plan to manage a small business, also select the Business check box (most people will only need the Home categories). Click Save.

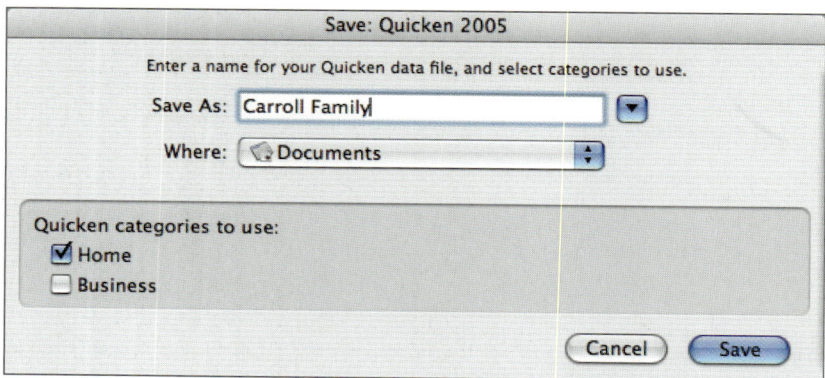

Quicken for Mac will then show you the New Account Assistant. You'll set up accounts in Chapter 2, so for now just click Cancel.

quicken for windows

The Quicken Home screen appeared when you finished with the Quicken Guided Setup. It's pretty blank now (because you haven't entered any of your accounts yet), but here's what it looks like when there's a bit more information in Quicken.

The menu bar contains the commands you use to accomplish tasks with Quicken.

The toolbar gives you an easier way to get to Quicken's features.

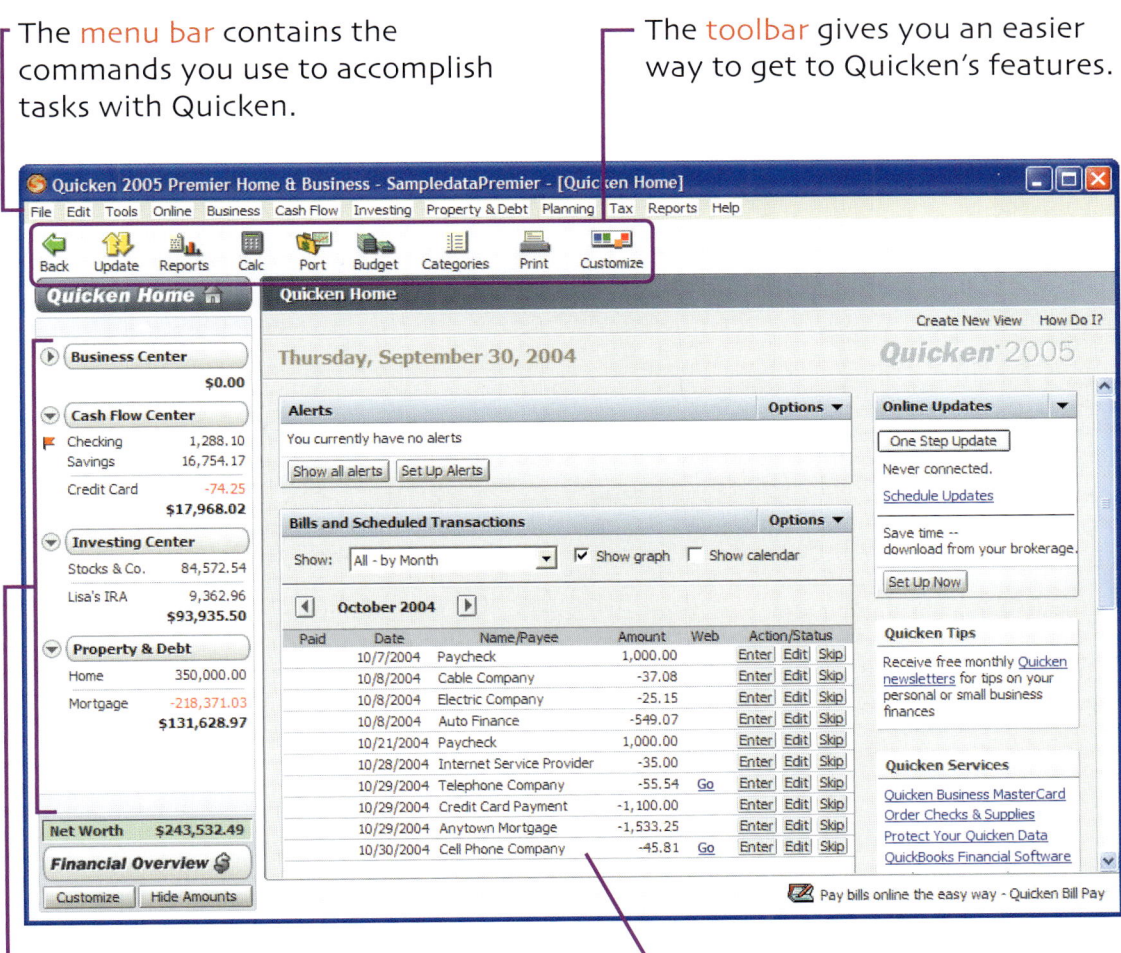

The Account Bar shows all your accounts, with their current values. You'll learn more about the Account Bar in Chapter 2.

The Bills and Scheduled Transactions list shows you upcoming financial events.

explore quicken   **5**

quicken for windows

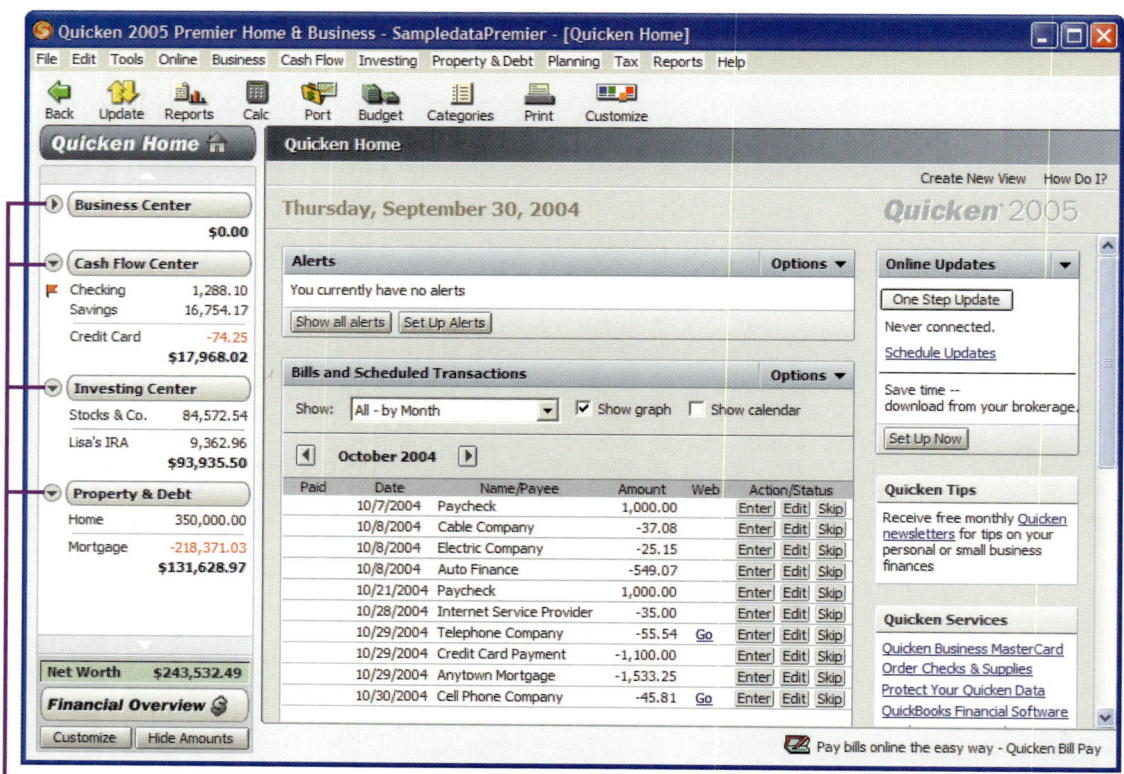

Quicken has several activity centers for different kinds of financial transactions; click on these buttons to display them.

Depending on the version of Quicken you're using (Basic, Deluxe, Premier, or Premier Home & Business), what you see may differ a bit from what is shown here (I'm using the Premier Home & Business version).

When you click on one of the accounts in the Account Bar, you see the register for the account. It looks much like your paper checkbook register, except that it's neater, and Quicken does all the math for you, giving you a running balance.

Checking	Register	Overview						
Delete Find Transfer Reconcile Write Checks Update Now					View ▼	Report ▼	Options ▼	How Do I?
Date △	Num	Payee		Payment	Clr	Deposit	Balance	
		Category	Memo	Exp				
6/29/2004		Telephone Company		67 00			1,997 17	
		Utilities:Telephone						
6/29/2004		Mortgage		1,200 00			797 17	
		Mortgage Interest						
6/30/2004		Safeway		45 00			752 17	
		Groceries						
7/1/2004	DEP	Paycheck				1,000 00	1,752 17	
		Net Salary						
7/1/2004		Deposit				1,000 00	2,752 17	
7/8/2004	Sched	Auto Finance		549 07			2,203 10	
		Auto:Loan	sports car					
7/15/2004	DEP	Paycheck				1,000 00	3,203 10	
		Net Salary						
7/21/2004	117	Dr. Siegler		240 00			2,963 10	
▶		Medical:Doctor						
7/30/2004	Num	Payee		Payment		Deposit		
		Category	Memo	Exp		Enter	Edit	Split
Online Balance:		750.40			**Ending Balance:**		2,963.10	

explore quicken

7

quicken for windows

Let's take a closer look at one of the transactions in the check register. Each transaction line contains all of the information about that transaction.

The Date field records when the transaction occurred.

Enter the check number or transaction type here.

The check's payee (or if it's a deposit, the source of the money) goes here.

For checks and other payments, this is the payment amount.

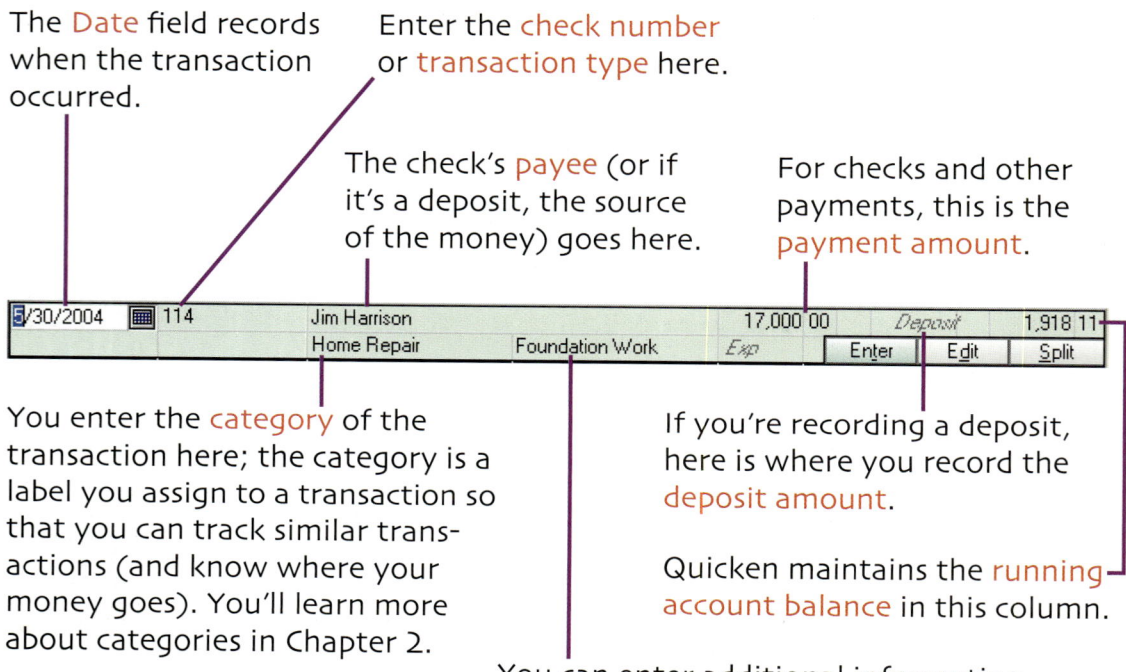

You enter the category of the transaction here; the category is a label you assign to a transaction so that you can track similar transactions (and know where your money goes). You'll learn more about categories in Chapter 2.

If you're recording a deposit, here is where you record the deposit amount.

Quicken maintains the running account balance in this column.

You can enter additional information about the transaction in the Memo field.

8 explore quicken

quicken for mac

Quicken for Mac has a similar user interface to its Windows counterpart, but there are some differences.

The menu bar contains the commands you use to accomplish tasks with Quicken.

You switch between Quicken's different financial areas with the activity area tabs.

The toolbar gives you an easier way to get to Quicken's features.

You can add custom account buttons to the toolbar.

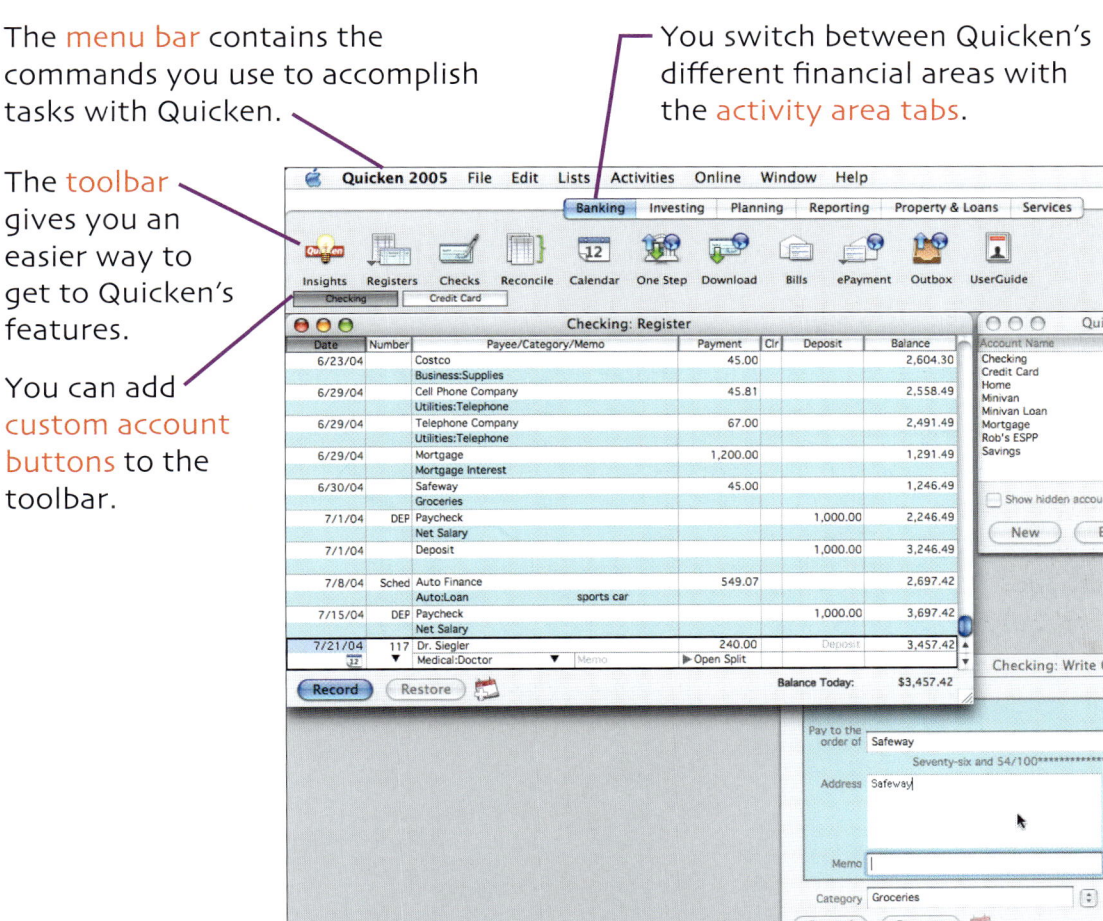

explore quicken   9

quicken for mac (cont.)

The Account List shows all your accounts, with their current values. You'll learn more about the Account List in Chapter 2.

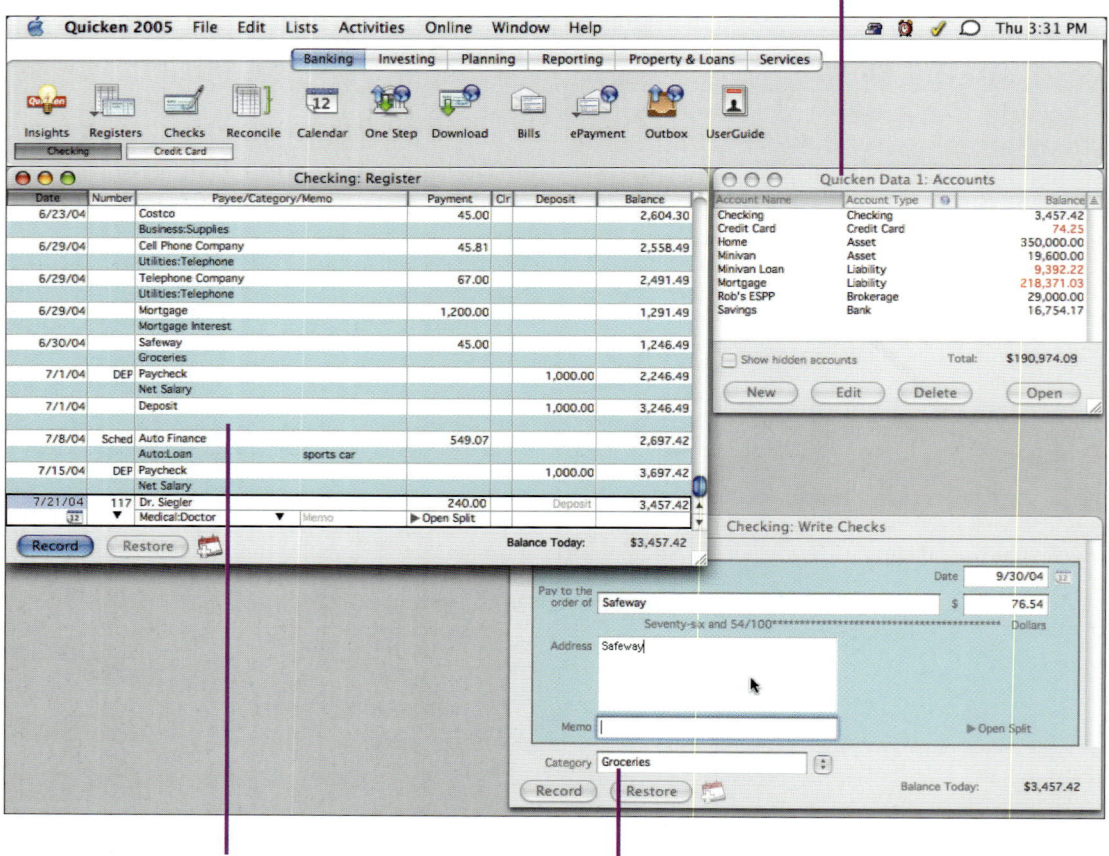

I've double-clicked the Checking account in the Account List, which opens its account register.

You can add transactions directly in the register, but sometimes the Write Checks window is more convenient.

Some transactions are assigned to more than one category; this is called a split transaction. You can spot these because they have split in the Category field of the register.

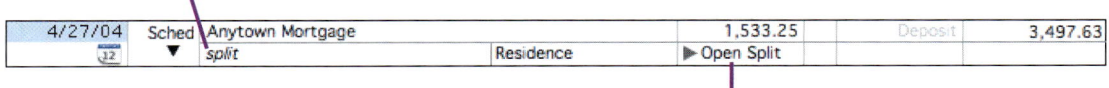

Clicking the Open Split button in the register shows the multiple categories. You'll learn more about split transactions in Chapter 4.

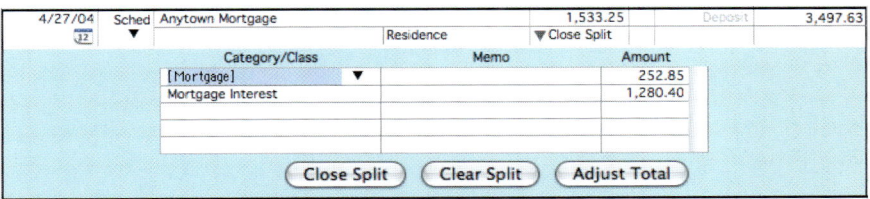

The Mac equivalent of the Windows' Quicken Home page is Quicken Insights, which gives you a good overview of your finances.

Account List

Expense graph

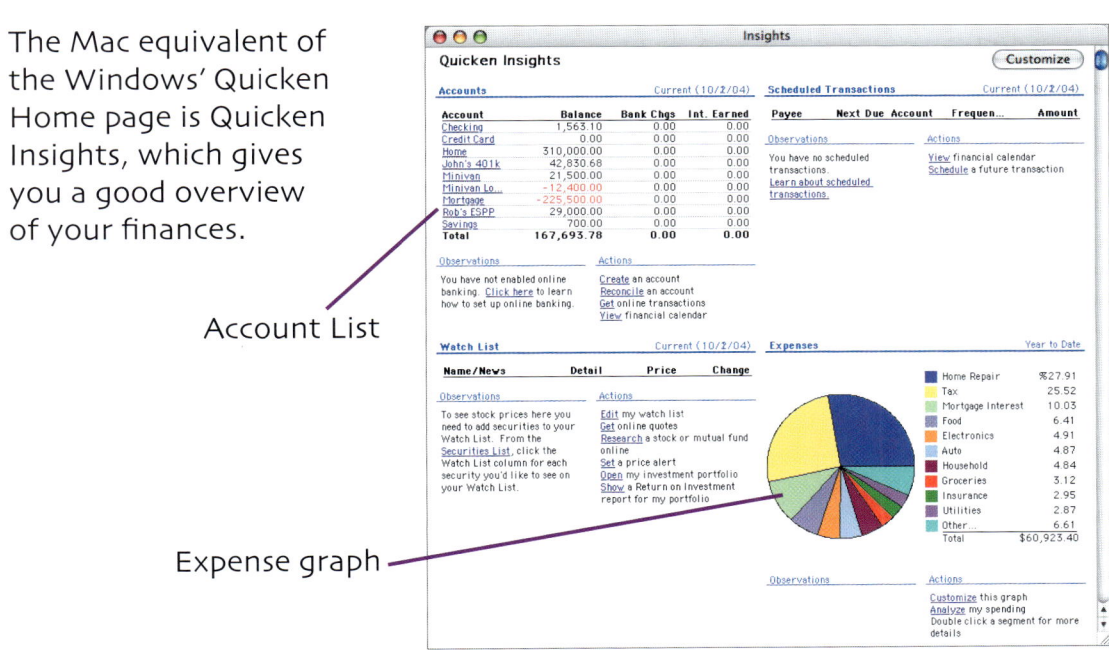

explore quicken 11

explore toolbars

On Windows, the default toolbar has a set of buttons that Intuit thinks will be the most useful for you.

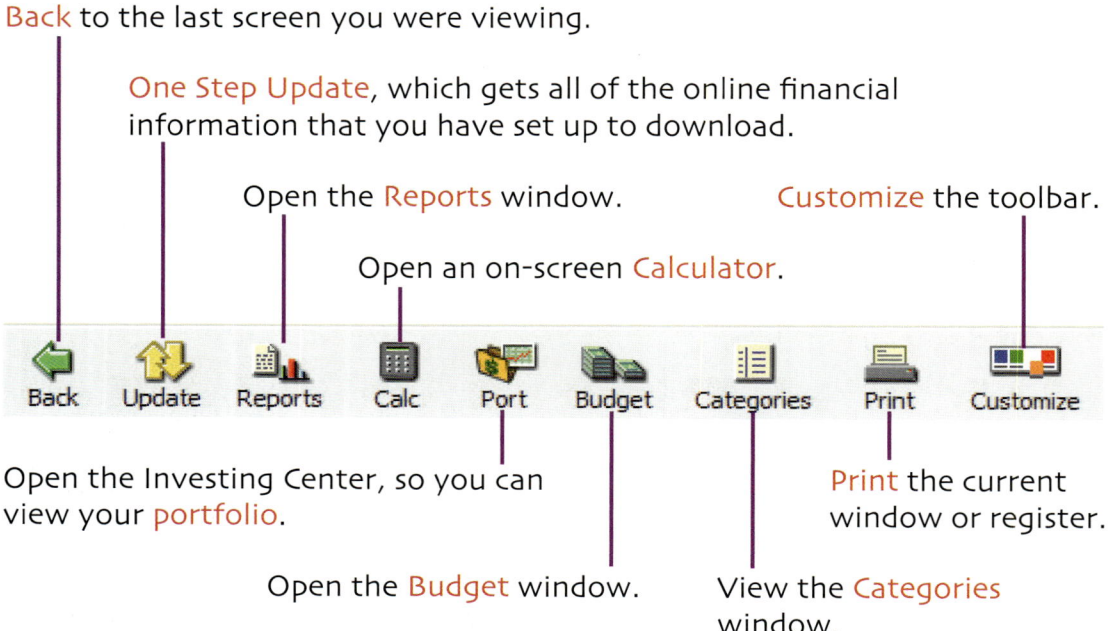

Back to the last screen you were viewing.

One Step Update, which gets all of the online financial information that you have set up to download.

Open the Reports window.

Open an on-screen Calculator.

Customize the toolbar.

Open the Investing Center, so you can view your portfolio.

Open the Budget window.

View the Categories window.

Print the current window or register.

Clicking the Customize button brings up the Customize Toolbar dialog. You can use the Add and Remove buttons to change the buttons on the toolbar, and the Move Up and Move Down buttons to modify button order.

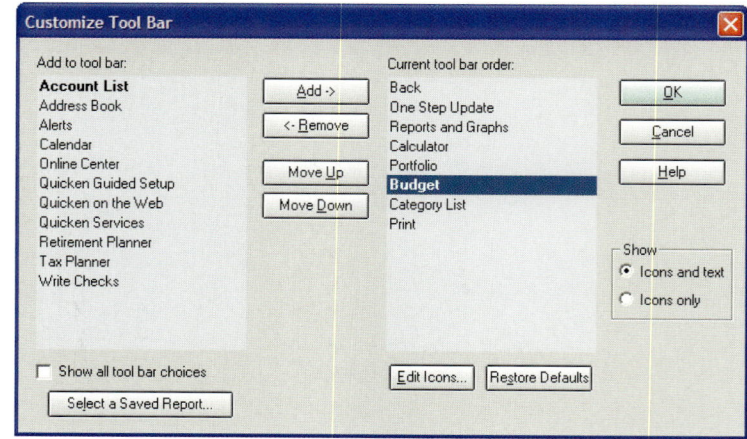

12

explore quicken

The toolbars on the Mac work differently; they are linked to their activity areas, and each area has a different set of buttons. For example, the Banking area has these buttons:

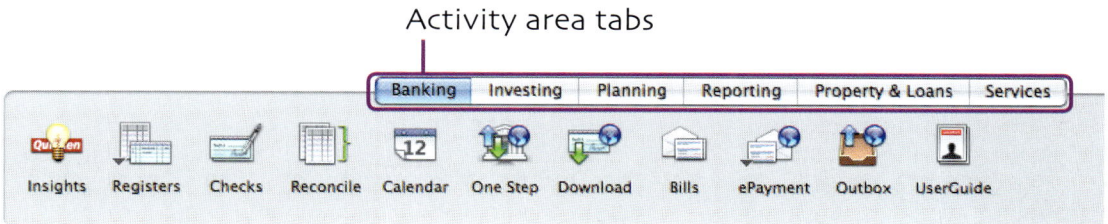

And the Planning area has these buttons:

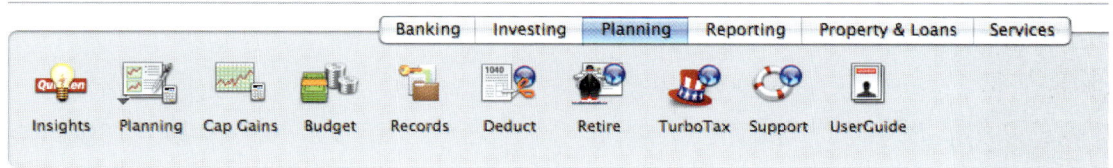

In all of the activity areas, buttons with a badge of the world, such as the TurboTax icon above, indicate online features that require an Internet connection.

explore toolbars (cont.)

You can also customize the toolbars on the Mac. Click the button for the activity whose toolbar you want to change, then choose Quicken > Configure Toolbar. The Configure Toolbar dialog opens.

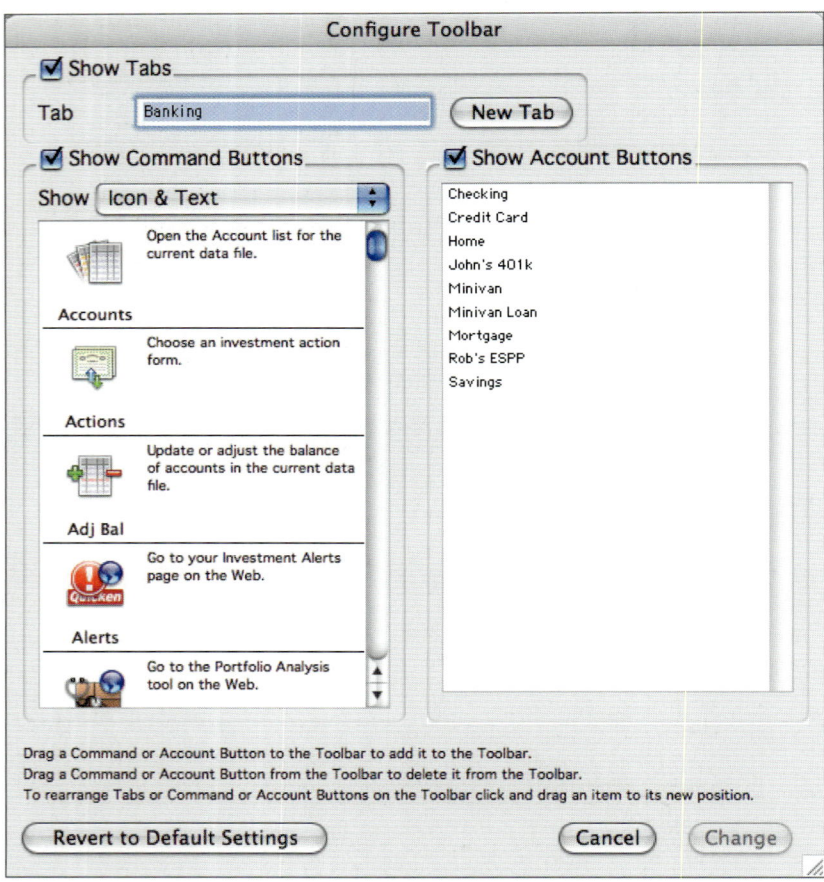

Follow the directions at the bottom of the dialog to modify the buttons, and then click Change.

explore quicken

extra bits

create data file (win) p. 2

- Here's a hard fact of life: Computers crash. Although they don't crash that often, it happens. Or your computer could become infected by a virus that trashes your files (especially on Windows). Besides computer problems, there are plenty of other things that can go wrong, including fires, mudslides, earthquakes, hurricanes—well, you get the idea. That's why you need to be thinking right now about backing up your data files.

A backup is a recent copy (or better yet, multiple copies) of your documents. If your computer has a CD-RW drive, you can burn backup copies onto rewritable CDs. Another good solution is to buy an external hard drive, hooking it up via FireWire or USB2.

No matter how you backup, you should get into the habit of backing up regularly. Establish a schedule. Get into the habit of backing up your files before you shut down your computer, for example. If you never shut your computer down, do your backup first thing in the morning when you're fresh; doing backups at the end of the day when you want to get away from the computer doesn't work as well.

Having multiple backup copies is the extra safe way to go. Keep one of your backups off the premises in a safe place, such as a safe deposit box. Bring in that backup and update it periodically—once a month, for example. Then take the backup off-site again. Having multiple backups does you no good if all of your backup disks are destroyed along with your computer.

explore quicken

extra bits

explore toolbars p. 12

- On the Mac, you can use the Configure Toolbar dialog to add custom buttons to the toolbars for your accounts, which makes it easier to open the individual accounts, instead of opening the Account List, then double-clicking the account name.

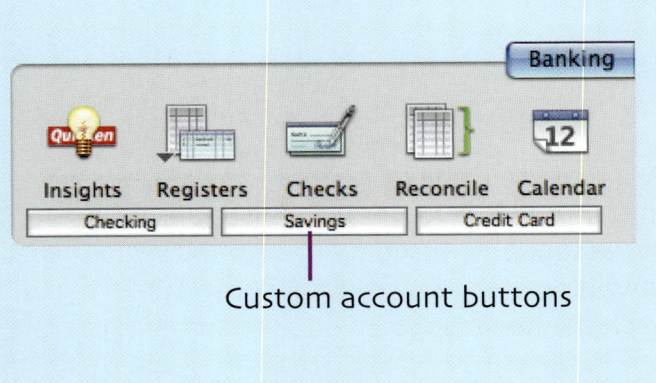

Custom account buttons

2. set up your finances

As you saw in the last chapter, Quicken stores all of your financial information in a single data file. Inside that data file, you'll create a number of accounts. An account represents an asset (something that you own, such as the money in your checking account or some property) or a liability (a debt that you owe, such as the balance on your credit cards or the mortgage on your home).

Quicken allows you to have as many or as few accounts as you wish. Some people prefer to use Quicken to track only their main checking account, and other people create many accounts to track every aspect of their financial life.

In this chapter, you'll set up the different accounts that you will initially use; learn about the different account types in Quicken; and learn about categories, the most important tool you'll use in Quicken to manage your finances.

decide what to manage

Before you dive into Quicken, it's useful to spend a few minutes deciding what parts of your financial life you'll manage with the program. Though Quicken can handle every aspect of your finances, I suggest that you start with just a few areas, like your checking and savings accounts and the credit card you use the most. The reason is simple: You're making a transition from paper systems to a computerized one, and there's a bit of a learning curve and some information to enter into Quicken. I'll help you with that learning process, and you can help yourself by not trying to enter in every last bit of your financial information at one time. As you become more comfortable using Quicken, and as you discover its benefits, you can add more accounts and manage more of your financial life in the program.

This is a great time to sit down for a moment with a pen and paper and jot down two short lists. At the top of the first list, write "This is what I want to do with Quicken." Then give yourself some clear, short goals, things like "Manage my checkbook" and "Pay my bills." As we work through this book, you'll make these goals happen.

In the second list, write down the names of the accounts you have chosen to set up now in Quicken. If you have only one checking account, it's OK to use the name "Checking" in Quicken. But if you want to manage more than one checking account, it's a good idea to give each a descriptive name, such as "Jim's Checking" and "Susan's Checking."

set up accounts (Win)

Let's set up your accounts in Quicken for Windows, including your main checking account, savings account (if you have one), and a credit card account (ditto). If you have them, get the last paper statements from each of these accounts. If you don't have them, that's OK; you can make changes later.

On Windows, you saw the Quicken Home screen when you finished with the Quicken Guided Setup in Chapter 1. In the Account Bar, click the Cash Flow Center button. The window changes to display the Cash Flow Center.

Let's add your main checking account. In the Spending & Savings Accounts section, click Add Account. The Quicken Account Setup window appears, asking you to enter the financial institution for the account (in other words, the bank where you have your checking account).

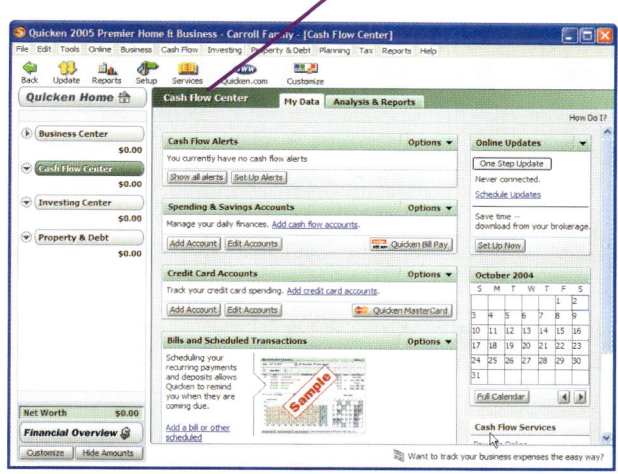

As you type the name, a pop-up list appears with choices. Keep typing until you find your bank. If your bank isn't in the list (unlikely, but possible), just type in the bank name.

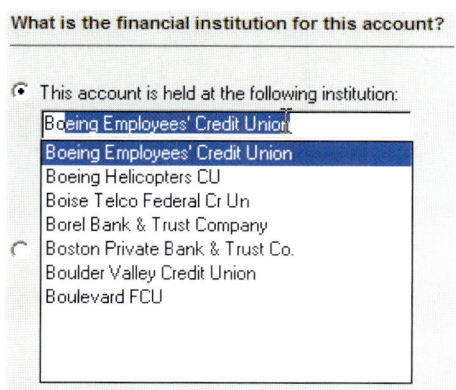

set up your finances 19

set up accounts (Win)

When your bank is selected, click Next. Quicken asks if you want to set up your account online or manually. Click Manual, and then click Next. (We'll cover setting up accounts for online access in Chapter 5.)

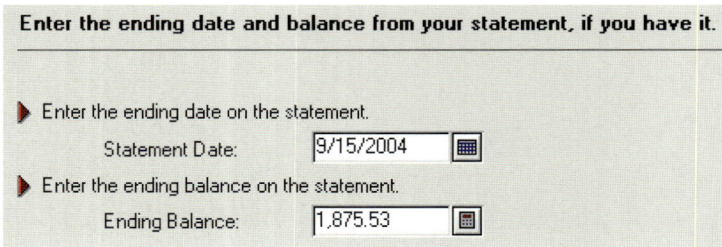

We're setting up a checking account, so click Checking on the next screen, then click Next. Give the account a name. If it's going to be the only checking account, then the default name of Checking is fine. Otherwise, give it a more descriptive name, so you can tell the different checking accounts apart. Click Next. On the next screen, enter the ending date from the last paper statement for the checking account and the ending balance, then click Done.

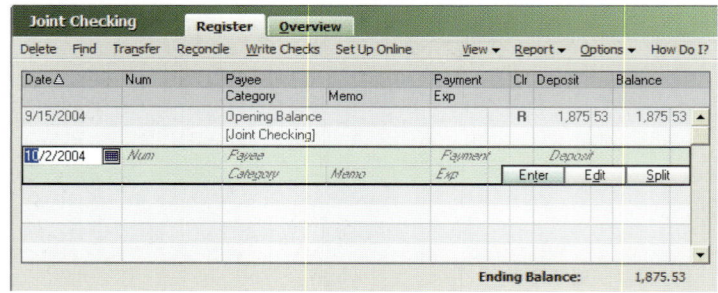

Quicken displays the register for your new account, with the opening balance filled in.

Repeat this process for the rest of the checking and savings accounts you want to set up.

20   set up your finances

To set up the credit card account, click the Add Account button in the Credit Card Accounts section of the Cash Flow Center. Follow the prompts to add the account information; it's much like adding the checking account.

As you finish setting up each account, it appears in the Account Bar and the Cash Flow Center. You also get handy totals of the amounts in your accounts, and for the credit cards, the amount of credit you have available.

set up your finances

set up accounts (Mac)

Let's set up your accounts in Quicken for Mac, including your main checking account, savings account, and a credit card account. If you have them, get the last paper statements from each of these accounts. If you don't have the statements, don't worry; you can make changes later.

If the Account List isn't open, display it by choosing Lists > Accounts, or by pressing Cmd-A. Then click the New button in the Account List. The New Account Assistant opens.

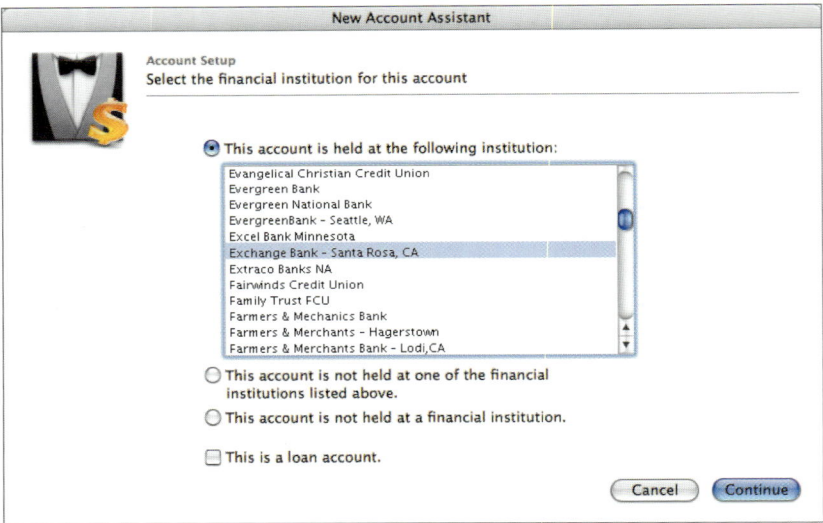

Let's add your main checking account. Type the first few letters of your bank's name to scroll the list of financial institutions, and then select your bank. If your bank isn't in the list, click This account is not held at one of the financial institutions listed above. Then click Continue. Quicken next asks if you want to set up your account online or manually. Click Manual, and then click Continue. (We'll cover setting up accounts for online access in Chapter 5.)

22   set up your finances

This screen shows the different kinds of accounts you can set up. Click Checking, and then click Continue. On the next screen, give the account a name. If it's going to be the only checking account, then the default name of Checking is fine. Otherwise, give it a more descriptive name, so you can tell the different checking accounts apart. Click Continue.

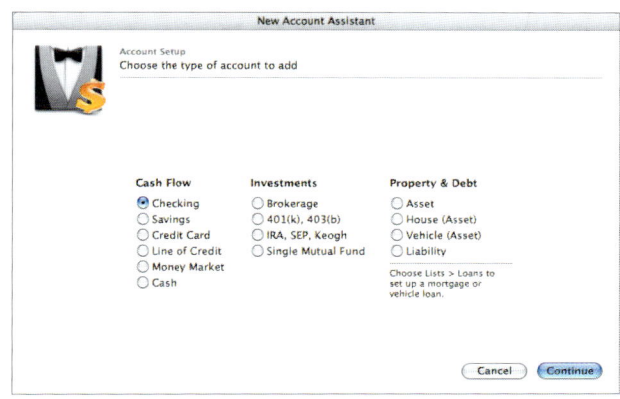

On the next screen, enter the ending date from the last paper statement for the checking account and the ending balance, and then click Continue. Quicken displays the register for your new account, with the opening balance filled in.

Repeat this process for the rest of the checking, savings, and credit card accounts you want to set up.

As you finish setting up each account, it appears in the Account List, with the balance for all your accounts.

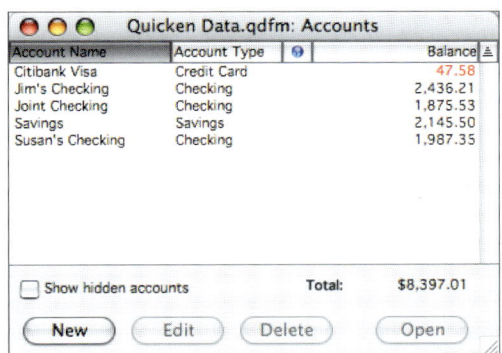

set up your finances   **23**

about categories

The whole point of using Quicken is to gain better control over your finances. To achieve that control, you'll need to know where your money comes from and where your money goes. You use Quicken's categories to track the flow of money. For example, when you buy food at the grocery store and record the transaction in a Quicken register, you can record it under the Groceries category. Later, when you're curious about how much money you spend on groceries, you can create a report that adds up all of your grocery transactions. You can—and should—assign a category to each transaction that you enter into Quicken.

By categorizing all of your transactions in Quicken, you can generate reports and graphs about the details of your income and expenses; save time and money while preparing your tax returns; and get a clearer view of your financial picture.

Because categories are used to track the flow of money, you need to be concerned about whether the money is flowing in or out. Money that is flowing in, such as your paycheck, is tracked using income categories. Money that you spend on your mortgage, utilities, groceries, and other bills is tracked using expense categories. A third type of category, the transfer category is used just to keep track of money that you move from one Quicken account into another.

You'll often want to track several types of income or expenses that are related to a single category. Quicken lets you use subcategories to handle these relations. For example, under the Medical category, you might have several subcategories for Doctors, Dentists, Prescriptions, and Insurance. Later, when you run an expense report, you'll be able to see just how much money you spent on each of the medical subcategories.

Quicken comes with a preset category list, but most people end up customizing their categories to better reflect their particular financial situation. For example, I write books for a living, and I want to know how much money each book brings in. So in my Quicken file, I set up a Writing category, and then I use the name of each book as a subcategory. At the end of the year, my income report shows me how much money each book brought in, and also shows the total for everything that is part of the Writing category.

set up categories (Win)

It's easy to add a new category or subcategory. The Carroll family lives in California, so they need to set up a subcategory for earthquake insurance. On Windows, choose Tools > Category List. The Category List opens.

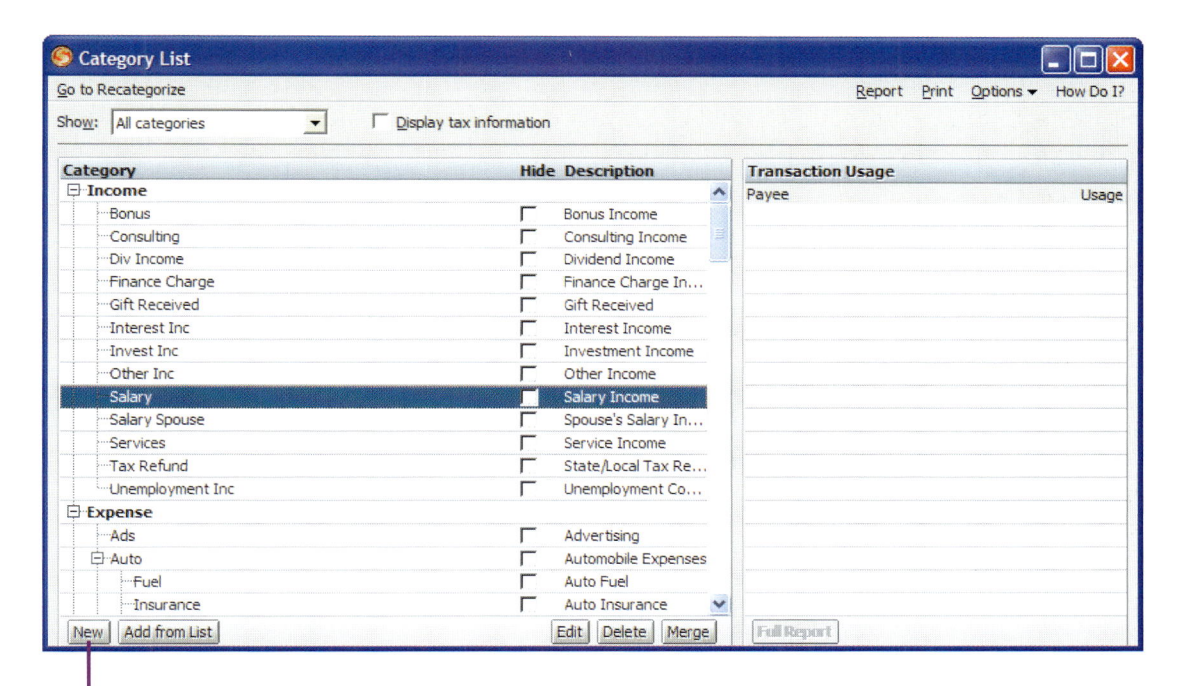

Click the New button at the bottom of the list.
The Set Up Category dialog appears.

set up your finances

set up categories (Win)

Give the new category or subcategory a name, then press the Tab key to get to the next field. Enter a short description. You can skip the Group field.

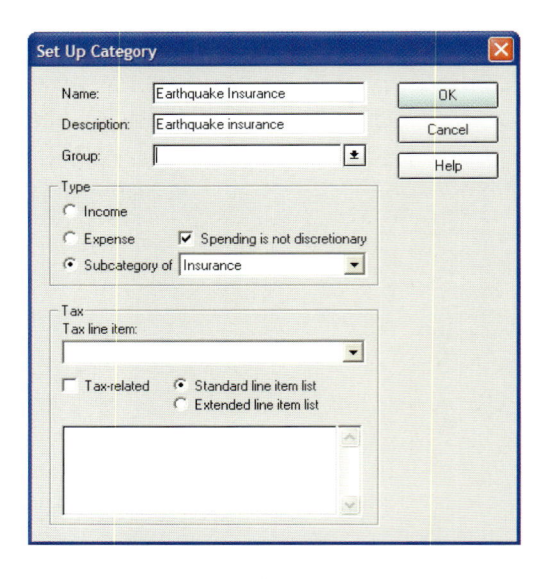

Next, click Income, Expense, or Subcategory of. If the latter, choose the parent category for the subcategory in the pop-up list.

If the category or subcategory is tax-related (meaning that you want to use it to track tax-related income or expenses), click the Tax-related check box, and choose the tax form line item from the pop-up menu that matches the category or subcategory.

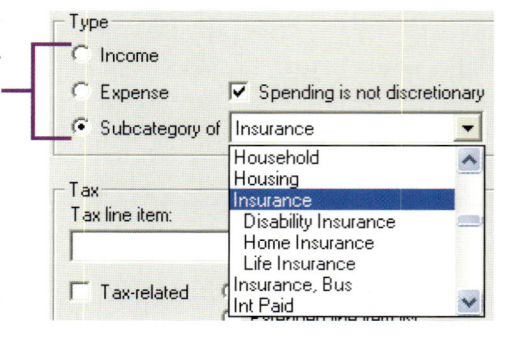

Quicken shows you a brief description of the tax form line item. For example, here is the Tax section of the IRA Contributions category. When you're done, click OK to save your new category or subcategory.

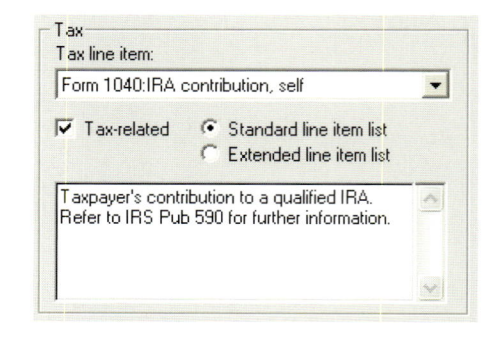

set up categories (Mac)

On the Mac, choose Lists > Categories & Transfers > List, or press Cmd-L. The Categories & Transfers List opens.

To add a category, click New. To add a subcategory, first select the parent category in the list, and then click Add Subcategory. In either case, the Set Up Category dialog appears.

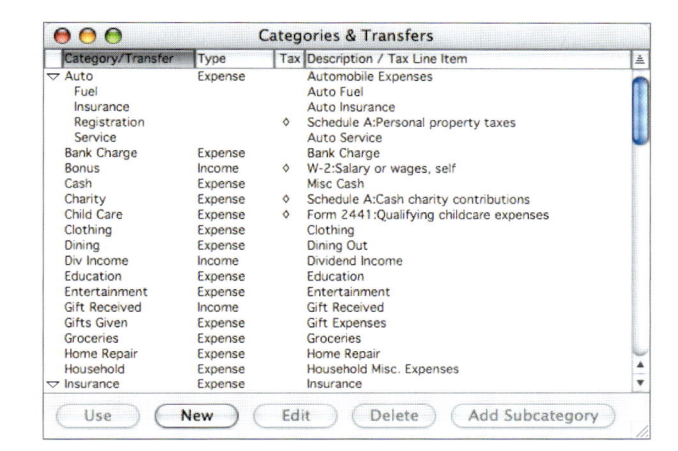

Enter the name and description for the category or subcategory. If you are adding a new category, choose the Category Type by clicking Income or Expense (if you're adding a subcategory, these buttons will be inactive, because a subcategory must always be of the same type as its parent category). If necessary, click the Tax-related check box. Then you can click Assign tax link and select the line item tax form for that category or subcategory. Click Create when you are done.

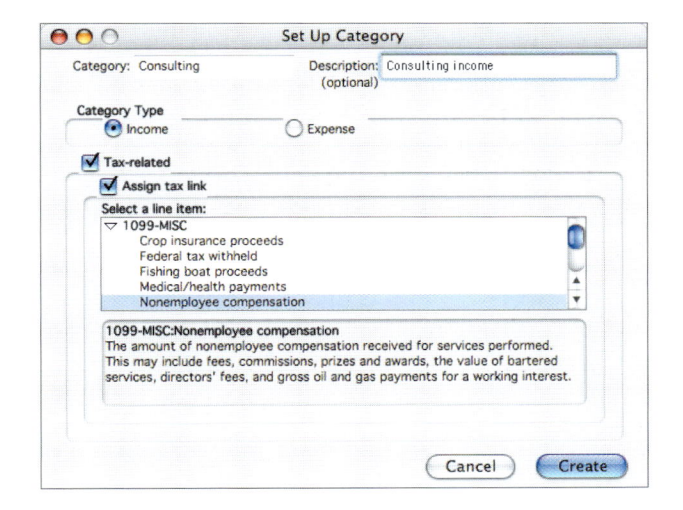

set up your finances   **27**

extra bits

decide what to manage p. 18

- The number one contributor to marital strife is disagreements over handling money. So it's a good idea to set up your finances to help minimize stress. Here's one proven way to manage a couple's finances: instead of having one joint checking account, use three checking accounts. Each person has his or her own account (to which their paychecks are deposited, which they can use for their own expenses), and each contributes an agreed amount every month to a joint checking account, which is used for shared expenses. This allows each person a certain amount of financial freedom, and both contribute to pay the common bills. Some couples contribute equal amounts every month; others contribute in proportion to the salary that each earns. Either way, it's a good way to handle a family's finances.

set up accounts (Win & Mac) p. 19

- Quicken allows you to have a Cash account, which is unlike the rest of the accounts because no corresponding account exists at a financial institution. You use a Cash account to track out-of-pocket expenses, or simply to record that spending money has come out of your checking account. For example, let's say that you withdraw $100 from an ATM. In Quicken, that amount comes out of your checking account and goes into the Cash account (because it is money flowing out of the checking account, it has to go somewhere). As you spend the money, you can make notations in the Cash account to track how that cash has been spent. This can be a useful exercise if you are having trouble figuring out how you spend your cash; keep really detailed records for a week or so, and you'll get a better look at your spending habits.

However, this may be more detail than you're willing to deal with; most people aren't going to keep receipts for small expenses like stopping at Starbucks in the morning. For my finances, I compromise; spending money comes out of my checking account and goes into the Cash account, but I don't bother to enter expenses in the Cash account. Naturally, Quicken thinks that the Cash account keeps growing (because there are credits and never any debits). This will eventually affect your net worth statement, because Quicken thinks that you're carrying thousands of dollars in cash in your pocket. I deal with this by occasionally entering a balance adjustment in the Cash account register, returning it to zero.

about categories p. 24

- It's important to use the same category names consistently throughout your Quicken accounts. For example, if you go to the doctor and pay with a check, you would enter that check under the Medical category in your checking account register. If on a subsequent visit you pay with a credit card, you would enter the transaction in your credit card account register using that same Medical category. This consistent categorization leads to accurate reports, and correct reports give you a better picture of your finances.
- If needed, you can create multiple levels of subcategories.
- If you delete a category, the transactions in your data file that were assigned to that category end up with no category at all. As a result, those transactions won't show up where you expect them in reports that are sorted by category and could be hard to find. It's better to try to avoid deleting categories altogether, but if you need to you should first reassign categories for the affected transactions using the Find/Replace feature in Quicken for Mac or the Recategorize feature in Quicken for Windows.

set up your finances

3. set up your paycheck

Now that you've set up your accounts and added categories, it's time to tell Quicken how to handle one of your most important financial transactions: your paycheck. Your paycheck isn't just a simple deposit; it's the amount you are paid (your gross pay) minus all of those deductions for taxes and other things like 401(k) contributions. You are left with your net pay, which is what gets deposited to your checking account.

Your paycheck is an example of a split transaction, which is a transaction that has amounts assigned to more than one category. Your gross pay is a positive number, say $1,000. Each kind of tax (Federal, state, Social Security, etc.) or other payroll deduction is a negative number. The remainder after deductions is your net pay.

On Windows, Quicken provides a handy wizard to help with your paycheck setup. On the Mac, you'll enter the different amounts into the register. On both platforms, you can memorize the paycheck and have Quicken automatically enter it for you the next time, so you only have to do the paycheck setup once.

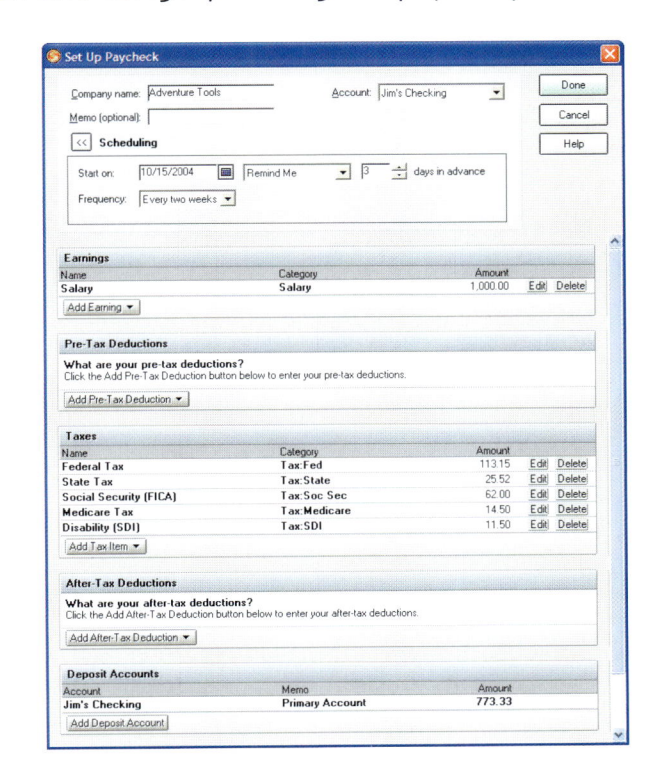

paycheck setup (Win)

To set up your paycheck so Quicken can use it, you'll need your latest paycheck stub. In Quicken, choose Cash Flow > Banking Activities > Set Up Paycheck. The first screen of the Paycheck Setup assistant appears. It's just informational, so click Next.

On the next screen, tell Quicken if this is your paycheck or your spouse's, then enter the name of your employer. Click Next.

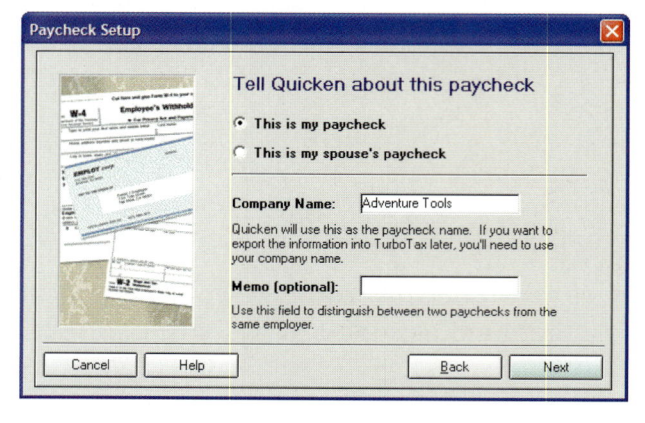

This next screen allows you to enter details of the transaction or just the net pay. Choose to track all earnings, taxes, and deductions, then click Next.

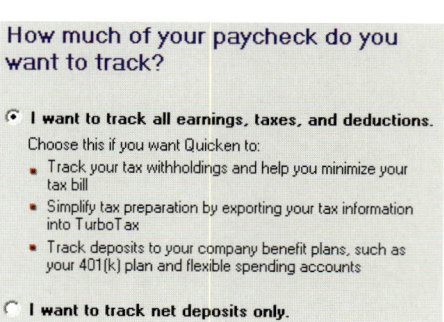

The main Set Up Paycheck dialog appears. It's a big dialog, so I'll show it in pieces as we work through it. At the top of the dialog, the Account pop-up menu shows the account to which the paycheck will be deposited. If the account is correct, move on; otherwise choose the proper account.

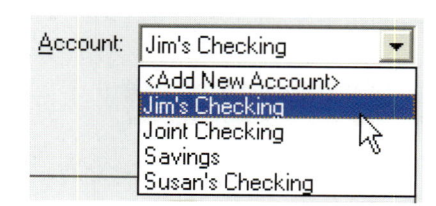

The Scheduling area is next. This allows Quicken to automatically enter your paycheck every pay period. Begin here by entering the date of your paycheck next to where it says Start on. You can type in the date, or you can click the calendar icon to get a pop-up calendar. Click a day in the pop-up calendar to enter it in the Date field. Next, choose Remind Me or Automatically Enter from the pop-up menu, and choose how many days in advance you want to be reminded to enter the paycheck. Depending on your choice, Quicken will give you a reminder that the deposit will be made, or will just enter it automatically in the register. If your paycheck is regular and the amount doesn't change from check to check, I recommend that you choose Automatically Enter here. If your paycheck amount varies, choose Remind Me; that way, when the paycheck arrives, you can change the split amounts in the transaction based on the amounts in your paycheck stub. Finally, choose how often you get paid from the Frequency pop-up menu.

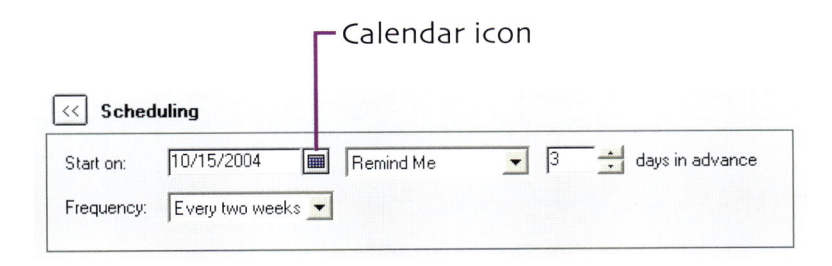

In the Earnings section, enter the gross amount of your salary, before any deductions. If you have other earnings that are included in the paycheck, such as a bonus, vacation pay, profit-sharing, and so on, choose the type of earning from the Add Earning pop-up menu. In the resulting Add Earning dialog, enter the amount, and then click OK.

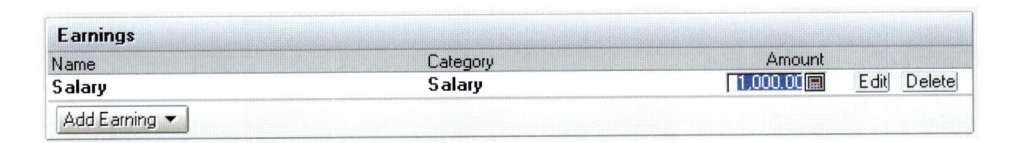

set up your paycheck   33

paycheck setup (Win)

Many people have deductions that are taken out before taxes, such as contributions to a 401(k) or other retirement account, or deductions for medical or dental insurance. If you have such pre-tax deductions, click the Add Pre-Tax Deduction button to get a pop-up menu with the possible choices.

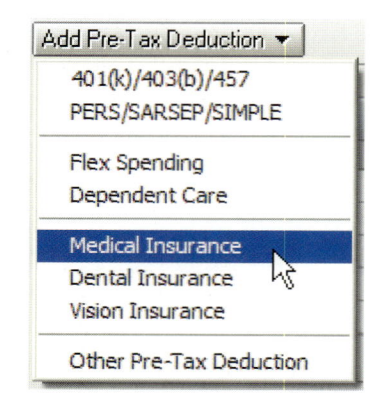

If you choose any of the first four choices, the Quicken Account Setup assistant starts up to help you create a Quicken account for the retirement or benefits plan you selected. Work through the assistant to create the account; you will return to the Set Up Paycheck dialog and will be presented with a dialog that allows you to enter the contribution amounts. For example, if you set up a 401(k), the Add 401(k) Deduction dialog appears. Fill out the dialog, then click OK.

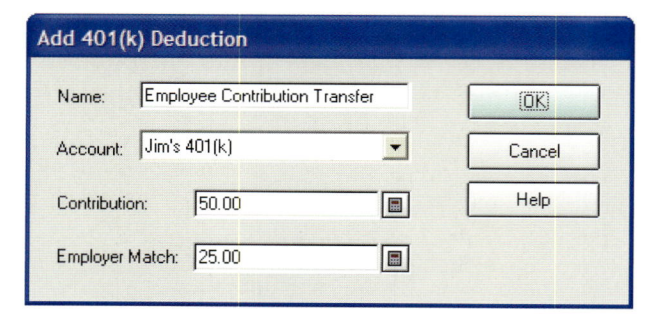

If you have other pre-tax deductions, add them now. Otherwise move on to the Taxes section, which is filled out for you with a standard set of taxes.

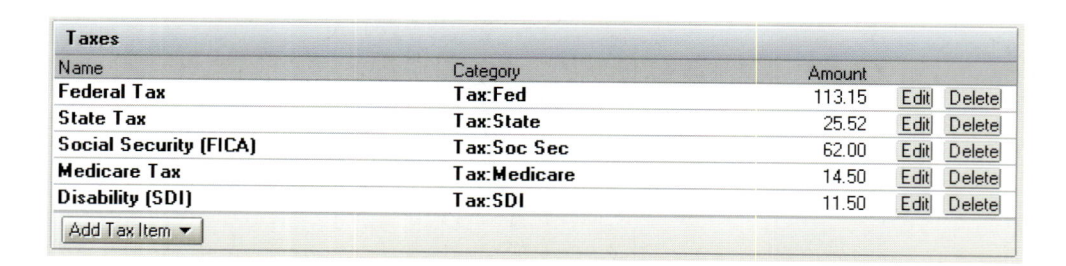

set up your paycheck

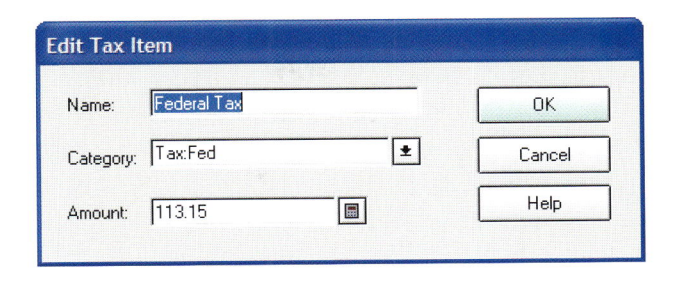

Click the Edit button next to each line item, and in the resulting Edit Tax Item dialog, enter the amount of that tax from your paycheck stub, then click OK. If you don't have some of the listed taxes (if, for instance, you live in a state with no state income tax), click the Delete button next to that line item. Continue through the line items until you are done.

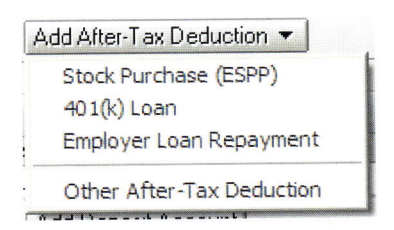

Some people have payroll deductions that are taken after taxes. For example, if you participate in an Employee Stock Purchase Plan (ESPP), you can purchase your company's stock with every paycheck. If you have such ESPP deductions, click the Add After-Tax Deduction button to get a pop-up menu with the possible choices, then work through the resulting dialog.

The bottom of the Set Up Paycheck dialog shows you the account to which the paycheck will be deposited, your net pay, and the W-2 Gross pay (the W-2 Gross is less than the Salary because of the 401(k) contribution, which comes off the top). You're done setting up your paycheck; at the top of the Set Up Paycheck dialog, click Done.

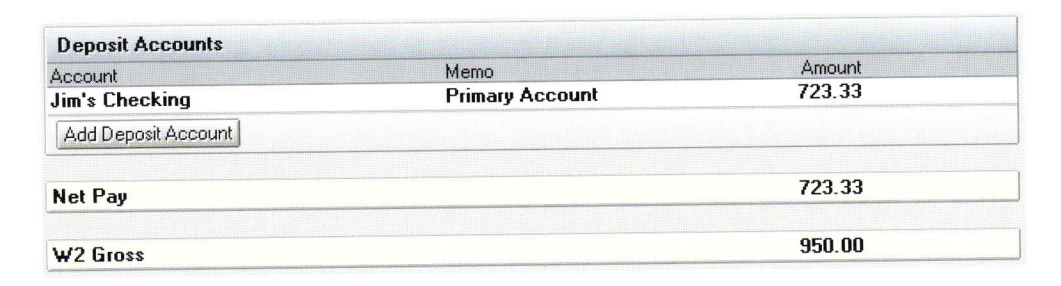

set up your paycheck

paycheck setup (Mac)

To set up your paycheck so Quicken can use it, you'll need your latest paycheck stub. You'll enter your paycheck information as a scheduled transaction, which is just a future transaction that you set up in advance, and that Quicken remembers so you don't have to enter all of the details each time. When the transaction comes due, Quicken either enters it automatically into your check register, or asks you if it's okay to add.

If you have pre-tax deductions from your paycheck, such as a 401(k) or other retirement plan, you must create that account before you begin setting up your paycheck. The same goes for post-tax deductions, such as Employee Stock Purchase Plans. See Chapter 2 for more information on setting up accounts.

Begin by choosing Lists > Scheduled Transactions. The Upcoming Bills and Scheduled Transactions window opens. Click the Scheduled Transactions tab.

Click New. The Enter Transaction dialog appears.

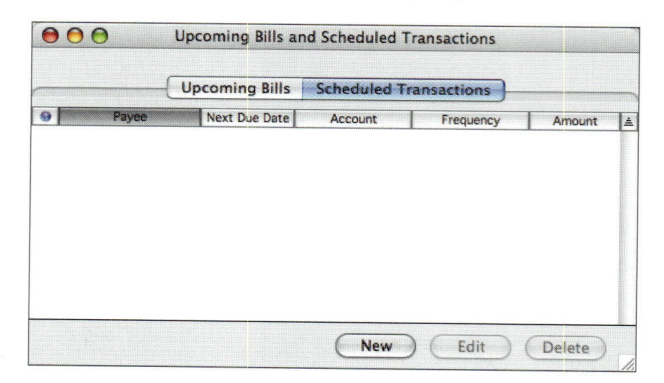

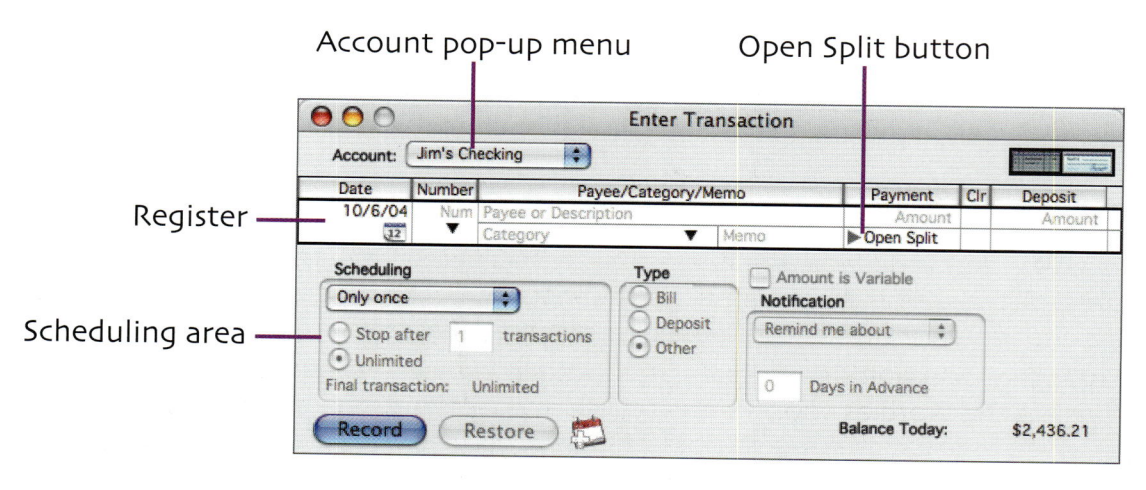

set up your paycheck

Check to make sure that the account shown in the Account pop-up menu is the one to which you want the paycheck deposited. In the Date field, enter the paycheck date from the pay stub. You can type in the date, or you can click the calendar icon to get a pop-up calendar. Click a day in the pop-up calendar to enter it in the Date field.

In the Number field, type d. Quicken will fill the field in with DEP, which means deposit. Press the Tab key to move to the Payee field, then type a description of the paycheck (I used Jim's Paycheck).

Now you'll begin entering the split transaction. Click the Open Split button to show the multiple lines for the split.

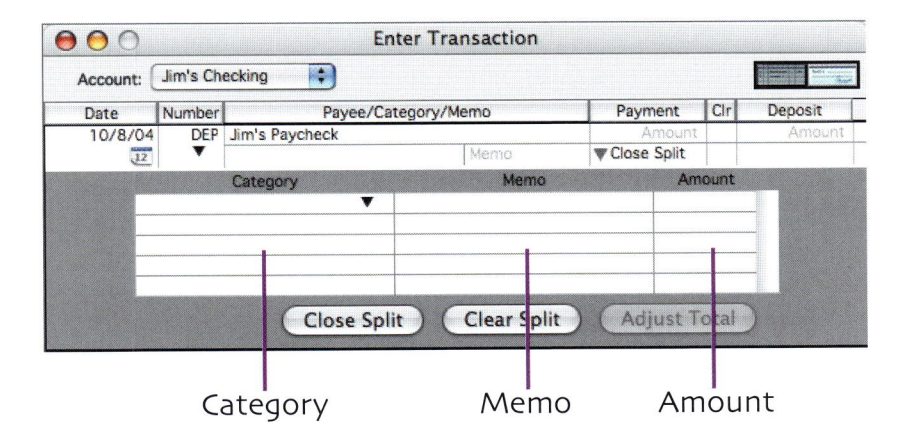

Category   Memo   Amount

The first line is for your gross pay. In the first Category field, type Salary, then press the Tab key until you are in the Amount column for that line. Enter the amount of your gross pay. Pressing the Tab key brings you to the next line. Note that you don't have to finish typing Salary; Quicken's QuickFill feature finishes the word as soon as you type a few letters. Quicken tries to make data entry easier for you whenever it can; for instance, if you enter a figure without a decimal point, Quicken puts the cents (.00) in for you.

set up your paycheck

paycheck setup (Mac)

The next several lines are for your paycheck deductions, such as 401(k) contributions and taxes. If you have a retirement account deduction, you need to show that money is going into the retirement account. You'll use a transfer category for this, which is a special category that Quicken uses to denote money flowing between two of its own accounts. Transfer categories always have square brackets [] around their names. Press the left square bracket, then begin typing the name of the retirement account. When Quicken finishes entering the name, press the Tab key until you are in the Amount field. Because this is a deduction, enter it as a negative number, so that it will be subtracted from your gross pay. For example, if the 401(k) contribution is $50, type -50.

Category	Memo	Amount
Salary		1,000.00
[Jim's 401k]		-50.00

Continue entering deductions on each line as negative numbers until you are done. Quicken scrolls the list of line items if needed.

Category	Memo	Amount
Salary		1,000.00
[Jim's 401k]		-50.00
Payroll Taxes, Self:Federal		-113.15
Payroll Taxes, Self:State		-25.52
Payroll Taxes, Self:Soc Sec		-62.00

Some people have payroll deductions that are taken after taxes. For example, if you participate in an Employee Stock Purchase Plan (ESPP), you can purchase your company's stock with every paycheck. As you recall from Chapter 2, a transfer category is used to keep track of money that you move from one Quicken account into another. Use the transfer category Quicken automatically created when you set up the ESPP account to denote the transfer of funds to the ESPP stock account and then enter the deduction as a negative number.

Finally, you'll set up the schedule for this transaction, so Quicken remembers it for you. In the Scheduling section, choose the frequency of the transaction from the pop-up menu, depending on how often you get paid. Click Deposit in the Type section. Under Notification, choose Remind me about or Automatically enter from the pop-up menu, and choose how many days in advance you want to be reminded. Depending on which you choose, Quicken will give you a reminder that the deposit will be made, or will just enter it automatically in the register. If your paycheck is regular and the amount doesn't change from check to check, I recommend that you choose Automatically enter.

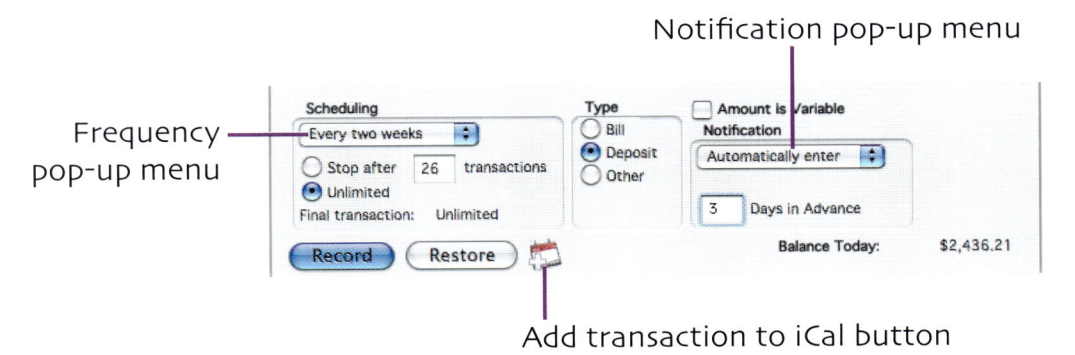

Notification pop-up menu

Frequency pop-up menu

Add transaction to iCal button

If you use Apple's iCal calendar program, you can add a reminder of the transaction to your calendar by clicking the iCal button. When you are done with the transaction, click Record. Quicken asks if you want to record the current transaction and future transactions, or if you are just creating a scheduled transaction for future transactions. If you choose Schedule future transactions only, Quicken will think that you are just creating a future scheduled transaction, and will not enter the instance of the paycheck that you hold in your hand. You need to enter the paycheck for which you have the pay stub, so select Schedule all transactions and click OK.

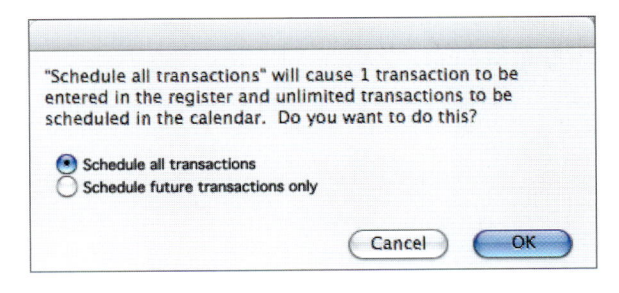

set up your paycheck 39

extra bits

paycheck setup (Win) p. 32

- It's possible to enter just your net pay into Quicken, but I don't recommend it. The reason is that there are real benefits to knowing the total amount of deductions from your paycheck, especially at tax time. You (or your accountant) can look at a report of all of the paycheck deductions and get the information you need to complete your tax returns more quickly.

- If your paycheck varies each pay period, you should still set up your paycheck as a scheduled transaction. You'll be able to enter the varying amounts in each split line without having to recreate them each time.

paycheck setup (Mac) p. 36

- The QuickFill feature is very useful to enter categories, but sometimes you need a quick list of all the categories to figure out which category you want to apply to the transaction. The triangle in the Category field of a register brings up a pop-up menu with all of the categories. Click the triangle, then choose from the pop-up menu.

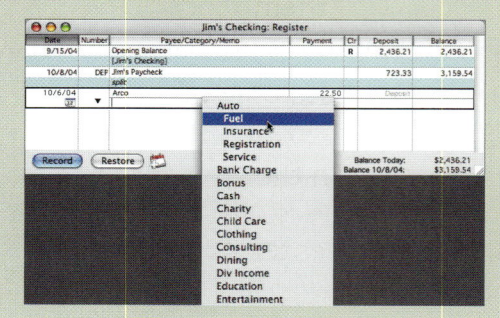

- Subcategories appear in the Category field separated by a colon. For instance, the Fire subcategory of the Insurance category would appear in the Category field as Insurance:Fire. When typing in the Category field, you can enter subcategories by typing the colon, then the first few letters of the subcategory.

4. write and print checks

On a day-to-day basis, you'll primarily use Quicken to handle the transactions in your various checking, savings, and credit card accounts. A transaction can be anything that changes the balance of an account. For a checking account, it could be writing a check, making a deposit, or withdrawing cash from the ATM.

Every account in Quicken has an account register in which you enter transactions. Quicken's registers look and act much like paper checkbook registers, which makes them familiar and easy to use. However, a Quicken register does the math for you and keeps a running balance automatically.

In this chapter, you'll learn how to enter transactions in the account registers, write checks, enter deposits, transfer money between Quicken accounts, and print checks from Quicken, rather than writing them by hand.

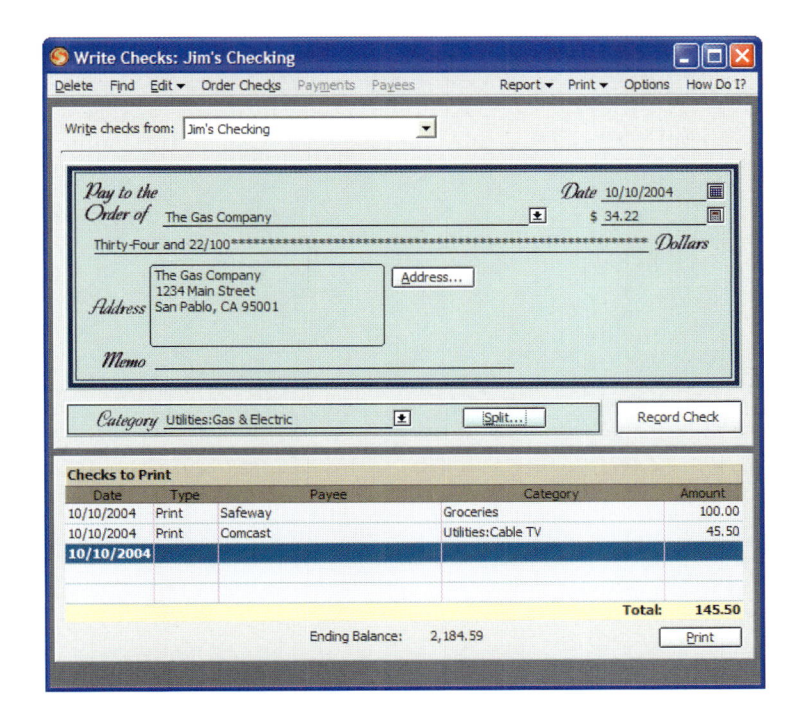

explore registers

Checks, deposits, and funds transfers from one account to another are all transactions that need to be entered in your account register. An account register uses boxes, called fields, to record all the information you need about the transaction, including the date, check number, payee, payment or deposit amount, category, and memo field. There's also a status box to indicate whether the transaction has cleared your bank or been reconciled with a bank statement. There is always a blank transaction at the bottom of the register, with labels to help you remember what information to enter. On Windows, there are also three buttons in the line item: Enter, which saves the transaction; Edit, which is a pop-up menu that offers you a variety of options; and Split, which opens the Split Transaction window (you'll learn more about splitting transactions later in this chapter). Account registers look slightly different, depending on the kind of account you are viewing. For instance, a credit card register uses Charge and Payment instead of Payment and Deposit.

Cleared/reconciled status box   Running balance

On the Mac, the register looks much the same, except that there is an Open Split button, and the button you click to save the transaction is called Record and is at the bottom of the register window.

enter transactions

To enter a check or deposit, first open the account by clicking it in the Account Bar (Windows). On the Mac, click the Banking tab and choose the account you want from the Registers pop-up menu in the toolbar.

The account register opens with the Date field highlighted and the current date filled in. If you want to change the date, type in a new date or click the calendar icon in the date field to get a pop-up calendar. Click to select a date in the pop-up calendar. You can also use keyboard shortcuts to enter dates. Press the Tab key to get to the Number field.

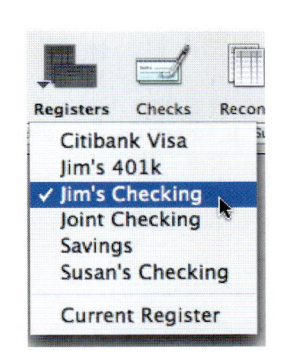

Press d (for deposit), and Quicken will fill in the field with DEP. You can use other keyboard shortcuts to enter transaction types in the Number field, or you can use the pop-up menu in the Number field.

Tab and enter the payee (for a check) or a description (for a deposit or transfer). Next, tab across to the Payment or Deposit field and enter the transaction amount.

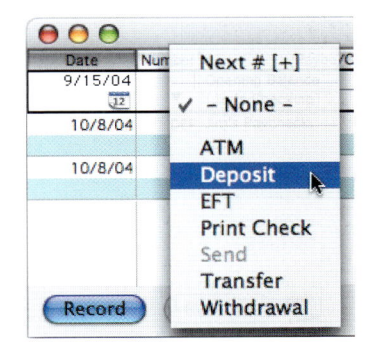

Press Tab to get to the Category field, then assign a category to the transaction by typing it into the field. The QuickFill feature fills in a category name from your list after you enter the first few letters. You can also use the pop-up menu in the Category field to select a category.

Optionally, in the Memo field, enter a memo about the transaction.

Press Enter (Return) to save the transaction and add it to the register.

10/9/2004	1452	Safeway Groceries	83 62		2,352 59

write and print checks

enter transactions (cont.)

date field keyboard shortcuts

shortcut	what it does
+	next day
-	previous day
t	today
m	beginning of the current month
h	end of the current month
y	beginning of the current year
r	end of the current year
[	same date last month
]	same date next month

number field keyboard shortcuts

shortcut	what it does
+	enters the next check number
-	subtracts a check number
a	ATM, an ATM transaction
d	DEP, a deposit
e	EFT, Electronic Funds Transfer
p	PRINT, a check to be printed
s	SEND, an electronic payment to be sent
t	TRANS, a transfer to another Quicken account

split transactions

Many transactions need to be divided among multiple categories. This is called *splitting the transaction*. For example, let's say that you write a check for both groceries and a prescription at a grocery store that has a pharmacy. You will want the grocery portion of the check recorded in the Groceries category, and the prescription portion recorded in the Medical category (of course, you can also split a deposit).

Let's enter a split transaction now. In the register, enter the date, check number, payee, and the payment or deposit amount. Click the Split button (Open Split button). On Windows, the Split Transaction window appears.

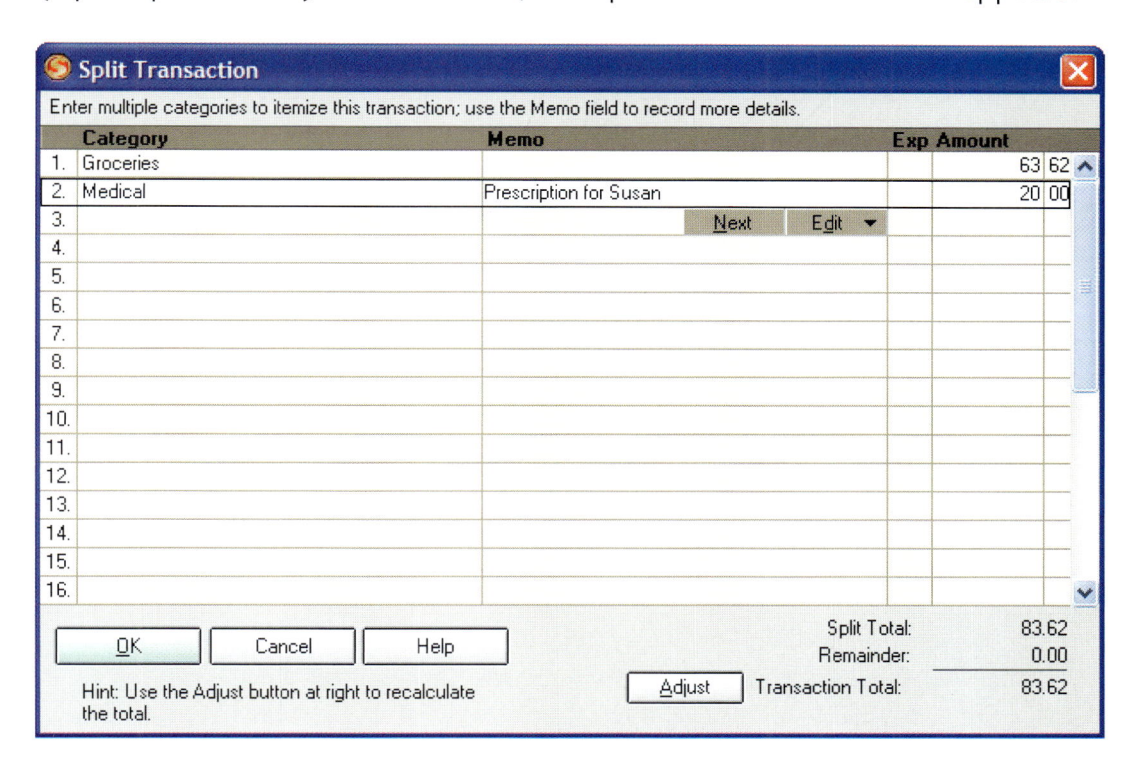

Enter the category in the first *Category* field in the split, either by typing it in or by choosing it from the pop-up menu.

Press the Tab key and (optionally) type a memo in the first *Memo* field.

write and print checks

split transactions (cont.)

Type the amount that you want to allocate to the first category in the first Amount field. Quicken subtracts that amount from the total and puts the remainder in the next Amount field. Enter the next category and amount on the next line. Repeat this until you have allocated the entire payment or deposit amount. Click OK to dismiss the Split Transaction window, then click Enter in the register to save the transaction.

On the Mac, clicking the Open Split button opens split lines in the register, rather than in a new window.

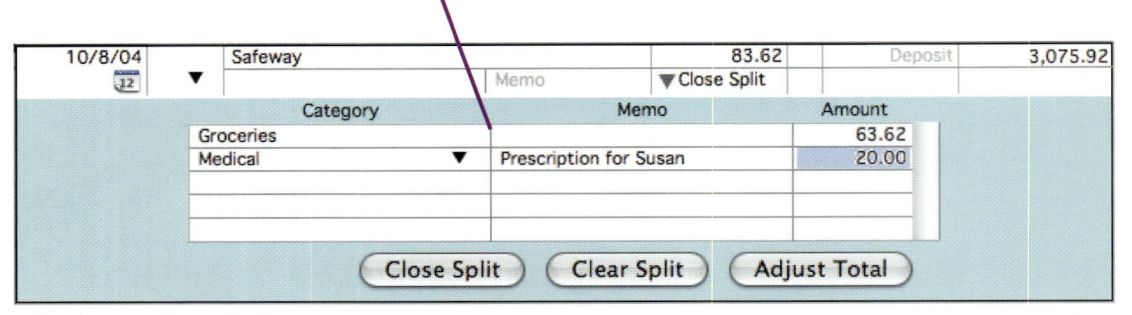

10/8/04	Safeway			83.62	Deposit	3,075.92
12	▼		Memo	▼ Close Split		
	Category		Memo		Amount	
	Groceries				63.62	
	Medical	▼	Prescription for Susan		20.00	
		Close Split	Clear Split	Adjust Total		

Follow the instructions above to allocate the amounts among the different categories in the split. When you have allocated the entire payment or deposit amount, click the Record button.

write and print checks

edit transactions

Unlike some other financial programs, Quicken allows you to make changes to transactions at any time, if you make a mistake in data entry. You can edit, delete, or void transactions whenever necessary.

To edit a transaction, open the account register that contains the transaction. Click the transaction in the register to select it, then in any field of the transaction select the incorrect information and type over it to replace it. Click Enter (Record) to save the changed transaction.

To delete a transaction, click on the transaction to select it, then choose Edit > Transaction > Delete (Edit > Delete Transaction). Quicken will ask you to confirm the deletion. Click Yes to delete the transaction.

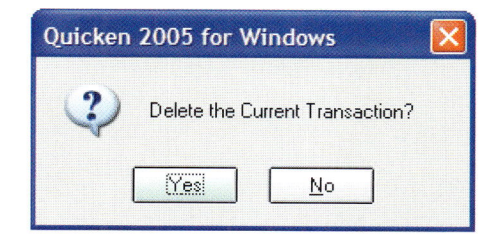

To void a transaction, click anywhere in the transaction to select it, then choose Edit > Transaction > Void Transaction (Edit > Void Transaction). Quicken places the word VOID at the beginning of the Payee field. Click Enter (Record) to save the transaction. Quicken removes the amount in the Payment or Deposit field and recalculates the account balance.

10/9/2004	1453	**VOID**Arco		Payment	c	Deposit	2,330 09
		Auto:Fuel	Memo	Exp		Enter Edit	Split

write and print checks   **47**

schedule transactions

One of the best ways to save time in Quicken is to set up scheduled transactions for recurring transactions that need to be paid on a regular schedule. Scheduled transactions can be entered automatically, saving you the drudgery of data entry. They are especially good for automatic deductions from your checking account, such as monthly service fees; because you don't initiate those kinds of transactions, it's easy to forget to enter them in your register. I also like to use them for bills that are the same from month to month, such as my cable TV bill.

Any transaction in your register can be turned into a scheduled transaction. You'll do the job a little differently on Windows and the Mac, but the idea is the same. On either platform, open the account register and click to select the transaction that you want to schedule.

On Windows, choose Edit > Transaction > Schedule Transaction. The Create Scheduled Transaction dialog appears.

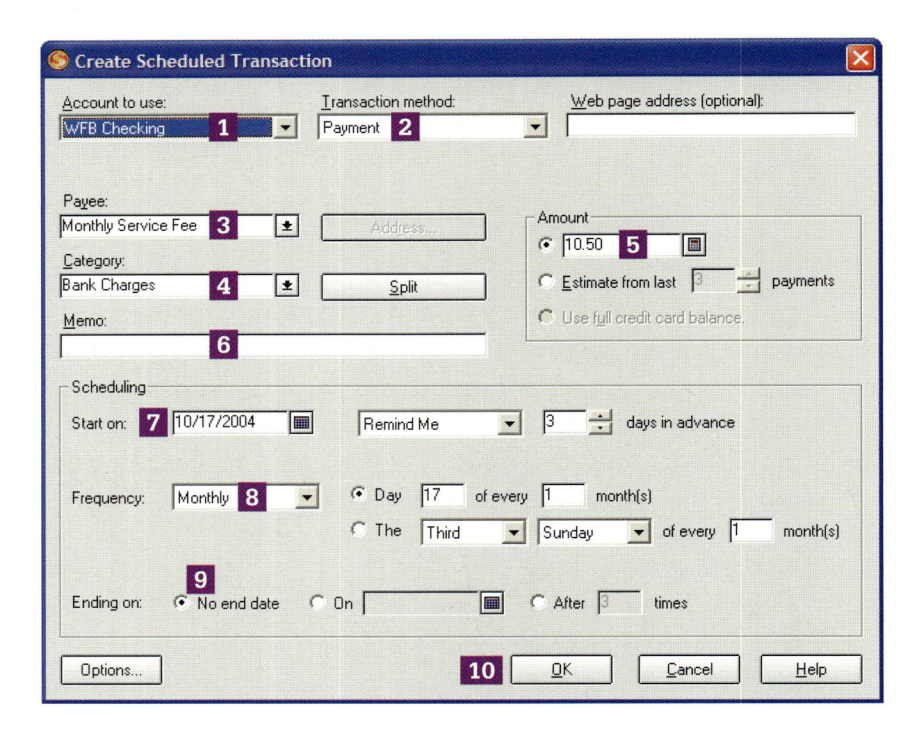

48   write and print checks

1 Pick the account from the Account to use pop-up menu.

2 The Transaction method can be Payment, Online Payment from Quicken, Printed Check, Deposit, or Transfer. Pick the one you want from the pop-up menu.

3 Type the payee in the Payee field, or choose it from the pop-up menu.

4 Type the category in the Category field, or choose it from the pop-up menu.

5 In the Amount area, if the transaction will be a fixed amount every time, click the first button and enter the amount. If the transaction amount is variable (i.e., it changes from month to month), you can have Quicken estimate an amount, so you have a rough entry in your register of the amount of the transaction. When you get the bill with the exact amount, you can edit the transaction to put in the actual payment. Click Estimate from last payments and choose how many payments you want Quicken to use for the estimate. If you are making a credit card payment, and want to pay the card balance off, choose Use full credit card balance.

6 If you want, enter a Memo for the scheduled transaction.

7 In the Scheduling area, enter the date you want the scheduled transaction to start in the Start on field, then decide if you want Quicken to give you a reminder of the scheduled transactions that you can enter yourself, or if you want Quicken to enter the transaction automatically in the register. You should also tell Quicken how many days in advance you want to be reminded of the transaction to be entered.

write and print checks   **49**

schedule transactions

8 Choose the Frequency of the scheduled transaction. This section changes depending on what you choose from the first pop-up menu.

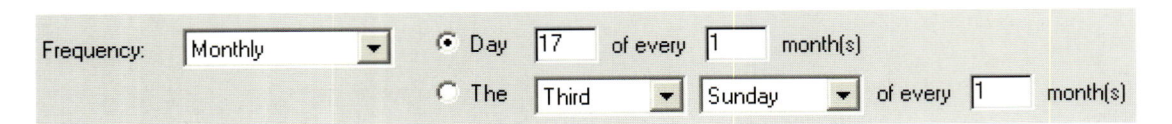

9 In the Ending on section, choose when Quicken will stop adding the scheduled transaction. You can choose No end date, to end on a particular date, or to end after a certain number of times (this last choice is good for loans).

10 Click OK to save the scheduled transaction.

On the Mac, choose Edit > Schedule Transaction. The Schedule Future Transaction window opens.

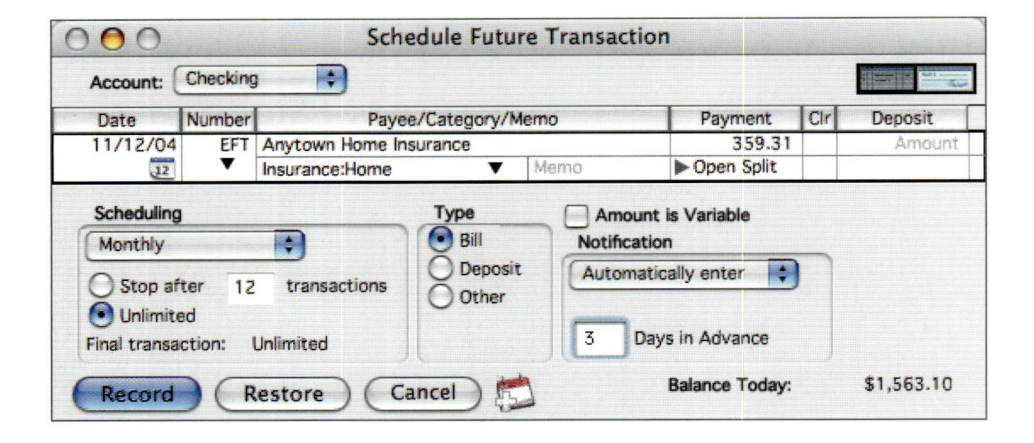

write and print checks

1 Enter the date you want the scheduled transaction to start in the Date field.

2 In the Scheduling area, choose the frequency of the scheduled transaction.

3 In the Type area, click Bill, Deposit, or Other.

4 Under Notification, choose Remind me about or Automatically enter from the pop-up menu, and choose how many days in advance you want to be reminded of the transaction to be entered.

5 If the transaction amount varies by a few cents from one time to the next, click Amount is Variable, and Quicken will show you and confirm the transaction each time before it is recorded in the register. If you check this box, the Notification pop-up menu will become inactive, because you will always be reminded, rather than having the transaction automatically entered.

6 Click Record to save the scheduled transaction.

transfer money

You often need to transfer money between accounts. For example, when you write a check to make a payment to your credit card account, money flows out of the checking account and into the credit card account, decreasing the credit card's balance. Quicken makes it easy to update both accounts with one transaction so you don't have to enter the same transaction in both registers. To accomplish this, Quicken uses a special kind of category called transfer categories, which refer to other Quicken accounts. Quicken creates transfer categories automatically when you create an account. You can view the transfer categories in your data file by choosing Tools > Category List (Lists > Category & Transfers > List) and scrolling to the bottom of the resulting window. The transfer categories are the ones enclosed in the square brackets [ ].

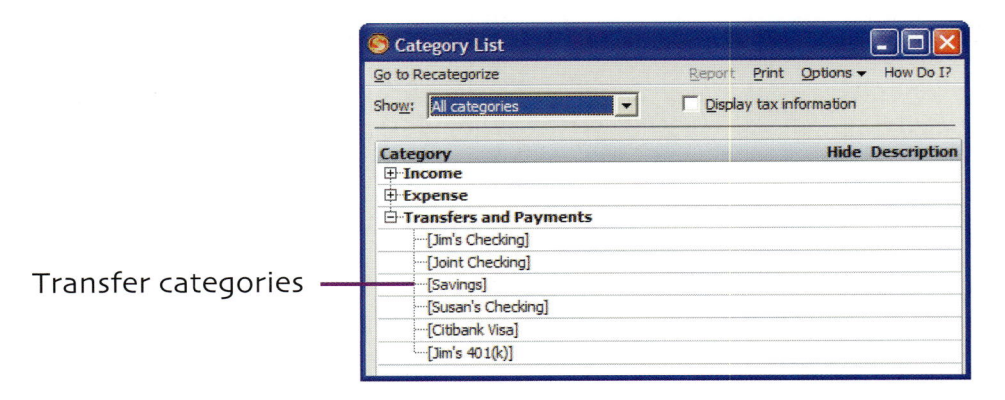

Transfer categories

On Windows, you'll find a Transfer button at the top of every account register.

Transfer button

write and print checks

Click the Transfer button. The Transfer dialog appears.

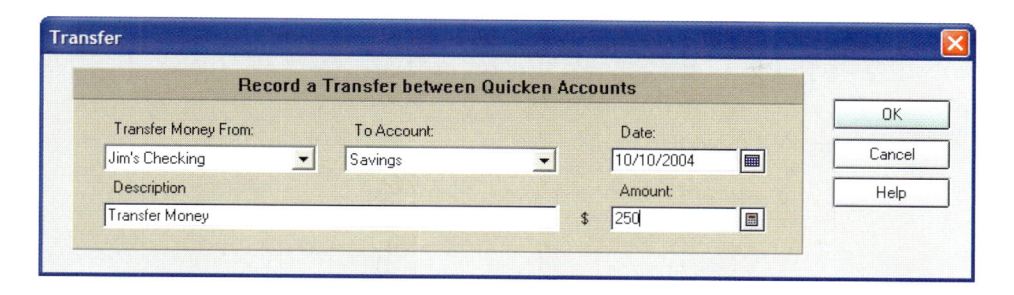

Using the Transfer Money From pop-up menu, choose the source account for the transfer, then choose the destination account for the transfer from the To Account pop-up menu. Quicken fills in the Date and Description fields for you, but you can change them if you like. Finally, enter the Amount of the transfer, then click OK.

On the Mac, choose Activities > Transfer Money > Between Registers. From the resulting dialog, enter the Amount and choose the From and To accounts. Quicken fills in the Date and Payee fields for you, but you can change them if you want. Click Transfer to record the transaction.

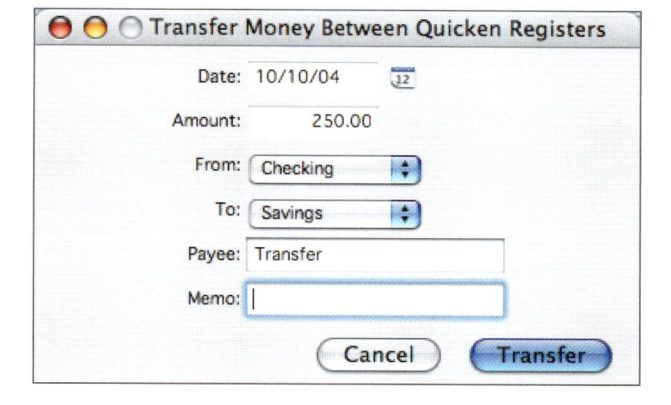

write and print checks 53

write checks

One minor drawback to using Quicken is that if you handwrite checks in your paper checkbook, you must reenter the check information into Quicken. There are two ways that you can avoid this double work. The most convenient is to use online banking and bill paying (see Chapter 5). You can also enter checks in Quicken, then print them onto preprinted check forms using your inkjet or laser printer. You'll need to order computer checks from your bank or a check printing company.

To set up a check to print, you can enter PRINT in the Number field when entering a check in the account register, or you can use the Write Checks window. On Windows, you'll find the Write Checks button at the top of the account register.

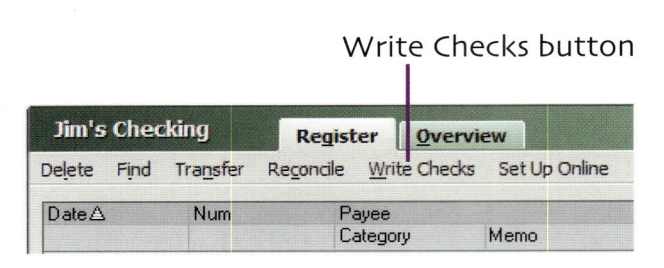

On the Mac, click the Checks button on the toolbar under the Banking tab.

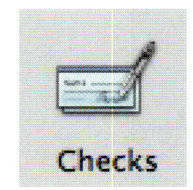

The Write Checks window looks like a real paper check, and you fill it out in much the same way. Enter the Date, Payee, and Amount. Quicken then turns the amount you enter into its text form on the next line. If you'll be using windowed envelopes to mail your checks, enter the name and address of the payee in the Address field. Otherwise, don't bother. Add a Memo if you like, then fill in the Category. Click Record Check (Record) to save the transaction and add it to the Checks to Print list (which only appears on Windows). When you're done entering checks, close the Write Checks window.

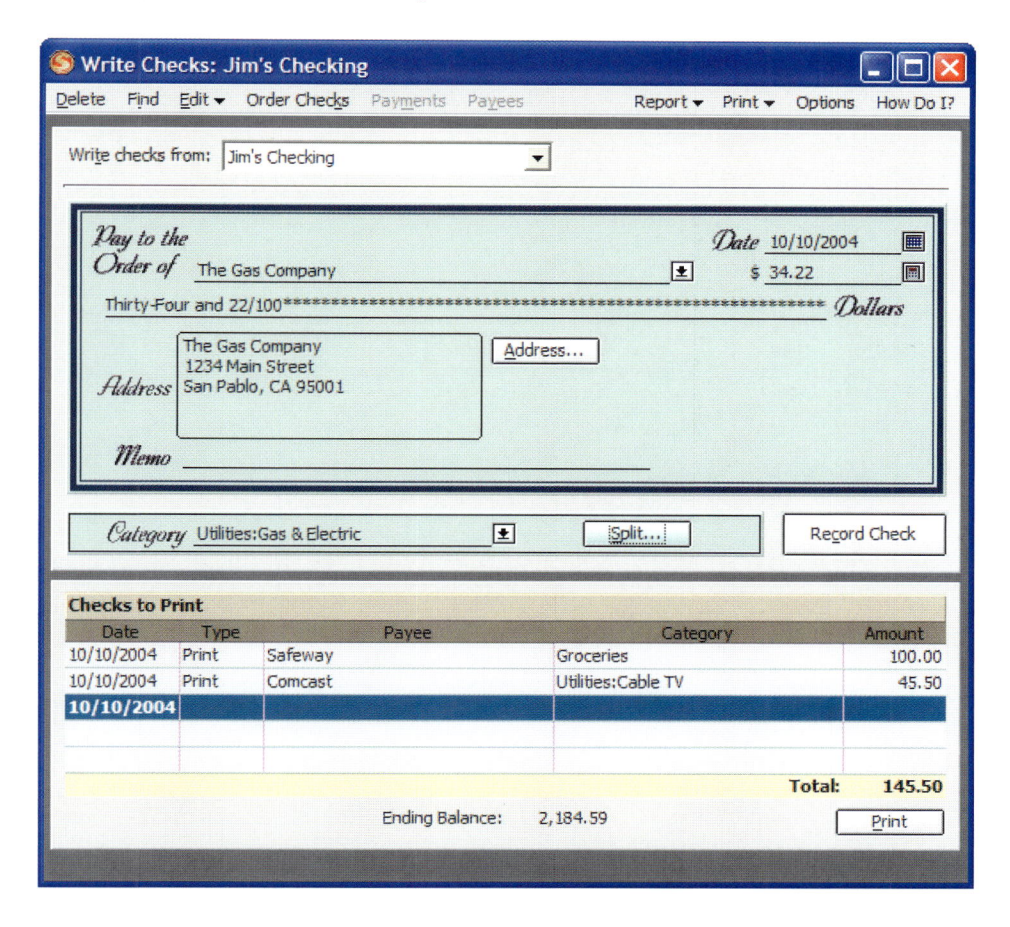

write and print checks   **55**

print checks

To print checks, make sure the checks are in your printer tray and positioned correctly for printing. You might want to run a test on some plain paper before you print on real checks for the first time. Verify that the printer is turned on and that it is online.

Choose File > Print Checks. The Select Checks to Print (Print Checks) window appears, telling you how many checks are ready to print.

The starting check number should match the first number of the checks that you put in the printer. If it doesn't match, change it. Click OK (Print) to print your checks.

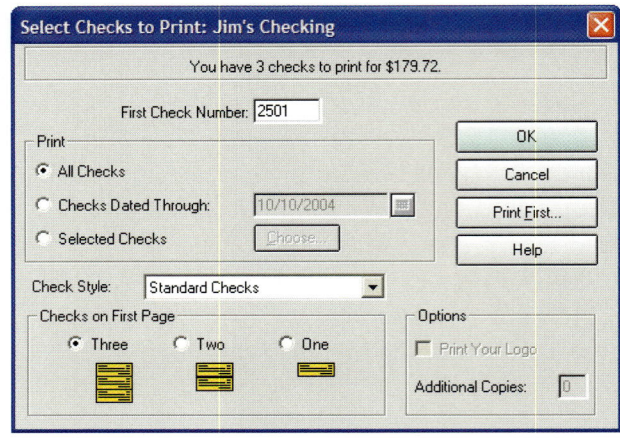

Select Checks to Print window (Windows)

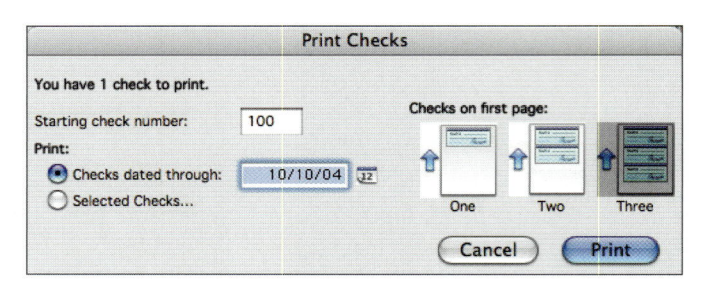

Print Checks window (Mac)

After the checks have been printed, Quicken will ask you whether all the checks printed correctly. If they did, click OK. If not, type the number of the first check which printed incorrectly, click OK and you will reprint checks from that number.

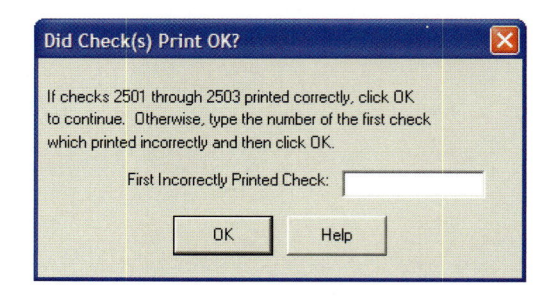

56   write and print checks

extra bits

enter transactions p. 43

- If you need to write a postdated check, simply enter a future date in the Date field. At the bottom of the register, Quicken will display the Balance Today and a future balance showing the balance as of the date of the postdated check.

- To quickly enter a date in the current month, type the day in the Date field and press the Tab key. Quicken automatically enters the current month and year.

- In any field in which QuickFill works, you can use the up-and-down arrow keys to scroll alphabetically through the possible matches. For example, if you type Hom in the Description field, QuickFill might guess Home Depot. Pressing the down arrow key would tell QuickFill to try the next possibility in the QuickFill list, Home Savings. Pressing the up arrow key scrolls up alphabetically through the list.

- Most of the time you'll want to keep your account registers sorted by date, but sometimes (like when you're trying to track down a particular check) you'll want to sort by the check number. Click the Date column header to sort by date; click the Number column header to sort by number. On Windows, you can also click the other column headers to sort by those fields.

- Sometimes it's useful to do a quick calculation while entering a transaction. For example, you might need to add up several checks when making a deposit. Quicken's QuickMath feature gives you a calculator right in the account register. QuickMath works a bit differently on Windows and the Mac.

    On Windows, most fields where you can enter numbers have a small calculator icon. Click the icon to pop up a calculator, then type numbers and click the arithmetic operator buttons to complete the calculation. The calculation's result appears in the number field when you're done.

    You can also access the calculator by pressing any of the arithmetic operator keys (+, -, *, /, or =).

    continues on next page

write and print checks

extra bits

On the Mac, in any field where you can enter an amount, press any of the arithmetic operator keys (+, -, *, /, or =) to pop up a "paper tape." Enter the numbers you wish to calculate, and press an operator key between each number. When you have entered all your numbers, click the Total button at the bottom of the paper tape or press Enter. Quicken places the calculation's result in the number field.

split transactions p. 45

- If you decide that you don't want to split the transaction after all, on Windows, click the Cancel button in the Split Transaction window. On the Mac, click the Clear Split button, which deletes all the information in the split lines.
- You can add as many lines of categories as you need to a split transaction.

schedule transactions p. 48

- On both Windows and Mac, you can view your scheduled transactions in a list. On Windows, choose Tools > Scheduled Transactions List. On the Mac, choose Lists > Scheduled Transactions.

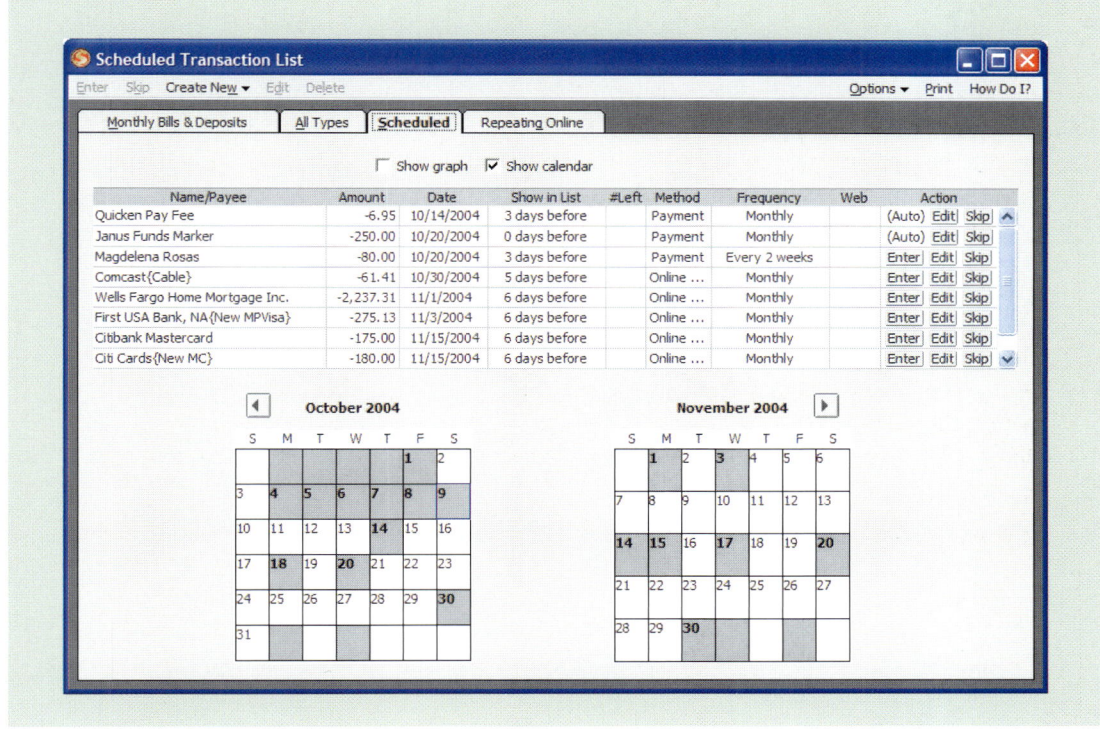

write and print checks 59

extra bits

write checks p. 54

- When you're away from home, you can write checks from the checkbook that your bank provided when you opened your account, or you can use your preprinted computer checks and fill them out by hand. I prefer to use my regular bank checkbook and enter the information into Quicken when I return home. I differentiate between the checks that Quicken prints and ones I handwrite by using two widely different sets of check numbers for each kind of check. For example, I started my computer checks at 1000 and my hand written checks start in the 4000 range. Quicken has no problem dealing with different sets of check numbers.

print checks p. 56

- You can buy preprinted computer checks from Intuit, but they're more expensive than other sources such as ASAP Checks (www.asapchecks.com) and Checks for Less (www.checksforless.com).

5. bank and pay bills online

The major portion of dealing with your finances is keeping your checkbook up to date and paying your bills. These tasks are probably not your idea of fun; they certainly aren't mine. So I'm ready to sign up for anything that makes these chores easier. Online banking and bill payment through Quicken doesn't make the job fun—heck, it's not a miracle cure—but it will make dealing with the bulk of your finances easier. You can save a lot of time and a bit of money.

Banking online saves you time because you don't need to record your checks, ATM withdrawals, or credit card transactions by hand. Instead, you download them from your bank, review the transactions to catch any possible errors and make sure they are properly categorized, then add them to your account registers with the click of a button. You can balance your checkbook in minutes every time you download your statement. Best of all, there's never any waiting in line when you're online.

Online bill payment lets you transfer money from your checking account directly to your creditors. You don't have to write or print checks, stuff envelopes, find stamps, or go to the post office. You simply enter a payment instruction in an account register and have Quicken send it over the Internet to your bank, which then transfers the money to your payees.

In this chapter, you'll learn how to enable your accounts for online banking and bill payment, download and compare transactions to your account registers, and pay bills and transfer money online using Quicken.

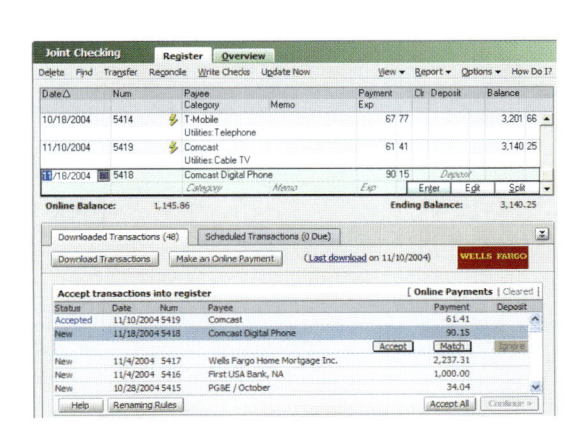

set up online accounts

To use online banking, you must first have access to the Internet, because Quicken uses the Internet to transmit and receive financial information from your bank. You must contact your bank or other financial institution (for example, a credit union or credit card company) to get online access for checking, savings, and credit card accounts. Not all financial institutions support online banking, and some support it only for certain account types, such as checking, but not credit card accounts. If you have accounts at more than one financial institution that you want to enable for online access, you'll need to apply to each one separately.

After you have signed up for online banking, your financial institution will mail you a kit with information to help you set up your Quicken accounts for online banking. For security purposes, this kit will usually be sent by U.S. Postal Service. You'll also receive an initial personal identification number (PIN), which you should change in your first online banking session. After you have received this kit, it's time to online-enable your accounts; that is, you'll set them up for online access.

To enable an existing account for online use on Windows, begin by selecting the account in the Account Bar. Choose Online > Online Account Services Setup. The Online Account Setup dialog appears. Click Edit Existing Quicken Account.

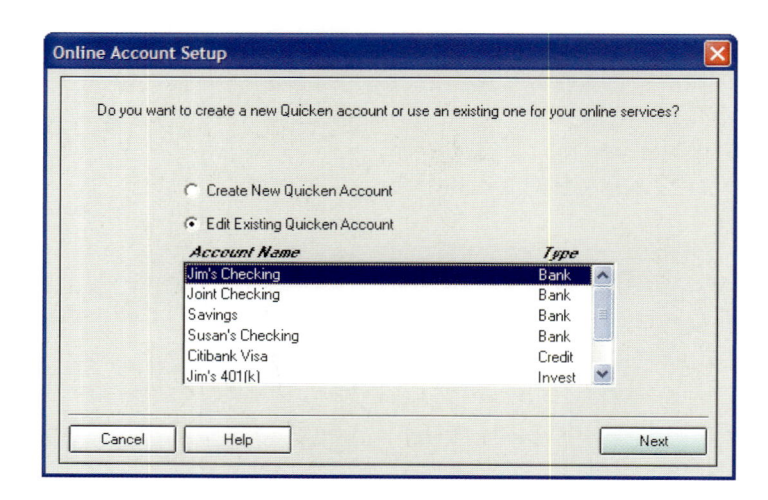

Select the account that you wish to online-enable in the scrolling list, and click Next. The login screen for your financial institution appears (you told Quicken the financial institution for the account when you created the account; see Chapter 2 for more details). Enter the information requested in the login screen, then click Next. In this example, Wells Fargo Bank uses the Direct Connect method, which requires my Social Security number (as the account name) and the PIN that the bank sent to me. Your financial institution may require different information.

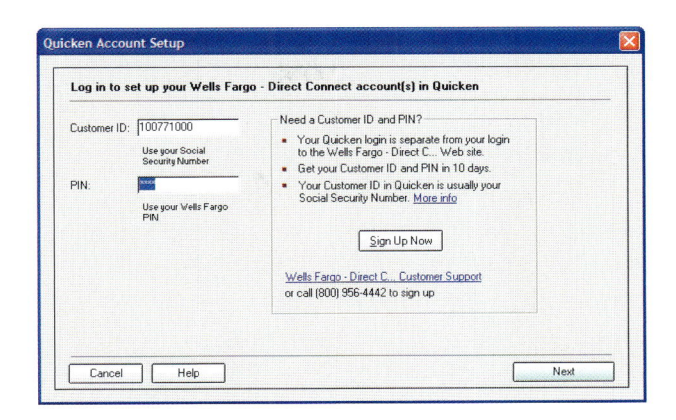

Quicken connects to your financial institution, and confirms that your account name and PIN are correct. Many financial institutions require that you change the PIN at this time, and will display a screen where you put in a new PIN. Enter and confirm the new PIN, and then click Next.

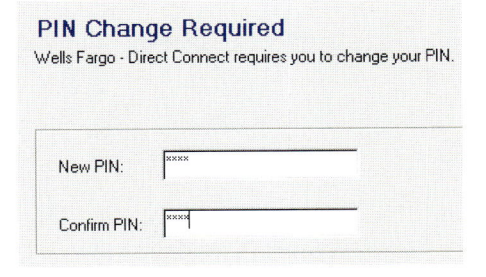

If you have multiple accounts at the financial institution, Quicken will detect them and ask which of the accounts you want to use. Choose the account from the pop-up menu, and then click Next.

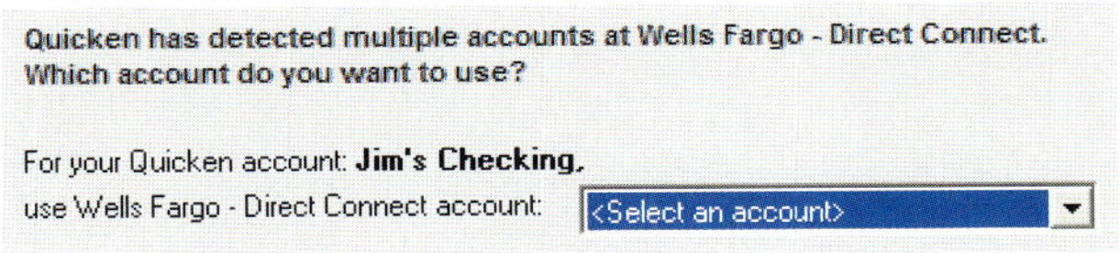

bank and pay bills online   **63**

set up online accounts

If there are additional accounts and your financial institution uses Direct Connect, Quicken may ask you to match the financial institution accounts with your Quicken accounts. If you don't want to do that, choose Do not use this account in Quicken from the pop-up menu. Otherwise, choose an account from the pop-up menu next to each account Quicken found, then click Next.

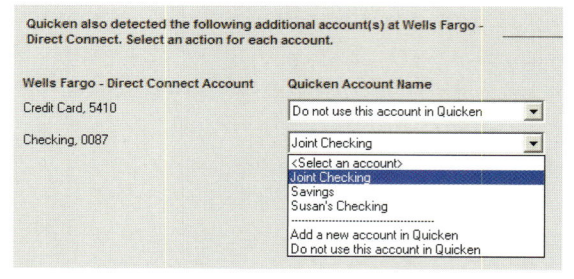

Quicken shows you a summary screen with a list of the accounts that you have online-enabled. Click Done. Quicken automatically connects to your financial institution and downloads all transactions from the last 60–90 days, then displays the Online Update Summary dialog.

See the compare transactions section later in this chapter to learn how to deal with the downloaded transactions.

To online-enable an existing account for the Mac, click the Banking tab on the Toolbar, then choose Lists > Accounts. The Accounts list appears.

Select the account you wish to online-enable, then click Edit. The account's setup dialog appears.

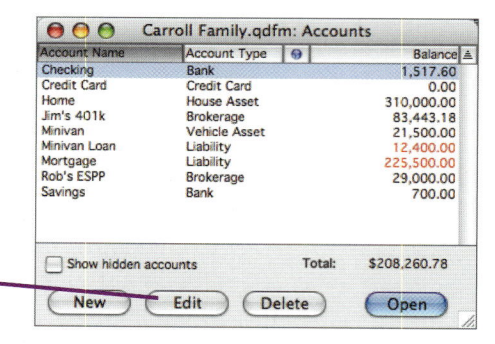

From the Financial institution pop-up menu, choose Select financial institution. Quicken will connect to the Internet and update the list of financial institutions, then will display the Financial Institutions window.

Scroll through the list to find your financial institution, click to select it in the list, then click Use. Quicken will ask for your Customer ID and PIN.

64   bank and pay bills online

Many financial institutions require that you change the PIN at this time, and will display a screen where you put in a new PIN. Enter and confirm the new PIN, and then click OK.

If you have multiple accounts at the financial institution, Quicken will detect them and display the Review Accounts dialog, asking which of the accounts you want to use.

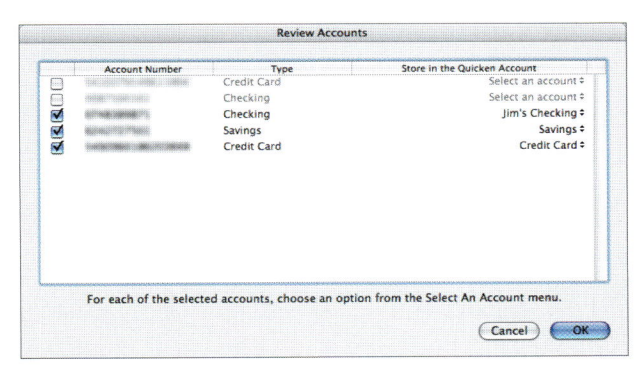

If you don't want to online-enable an account, uncheck it in the list. For accounts you want to online-enable, choose the Quicken account you want to associate it with using the pop-up menus in the Store in the Quicken Account column. When you're done, click OK.

Quicken connects to your financial institution and downloads the recent (60–90 days, depending on your institution) transactions for the selected accounts. The Download Transactions screen appears; see the compare transactions section later in this chapter to learn how to deal with the downloaded transactions.

bank and pay bills online

use Web Connect

If your financial institution supports the Direct Connect connection method to download transactions, you should always use that, as it is more convenient than Web Connect. But some institutions only support Web Connect, which uses a Web browser to connect to the financial institution's Web site, where you can then download a file containing your transactions. You then import the downloaded file into Quicken. On Windows, Quicken uses an embedded version of Internet Explorer to connect to the financial institution's Web site. On the Mac, you can use Safari or Internet Explorer. To use Web Connect for the first time, you will need to obtain a welcome kit from your financial institution, which will include a user ID and PIN.

To download transactions using Web Connect on Windows, click to select the account in the Account Bar, then click the Download Transactions button on the account register.

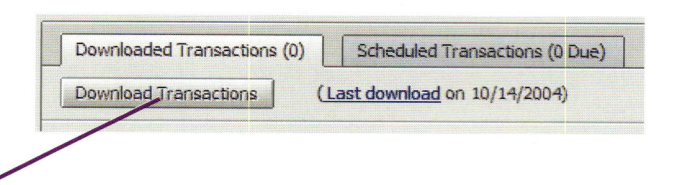

A new browser window will open to the login page of your financial institution's Web site. Enter your account name and password, and log in.

bank and pay bills online

Use the Web site to navigate to where you can download your account statement. Each financial institution's Web site differs, and they may call the option "Download statement," "Download account activity," or something similar. Follow the on-screen instructions to download the file.

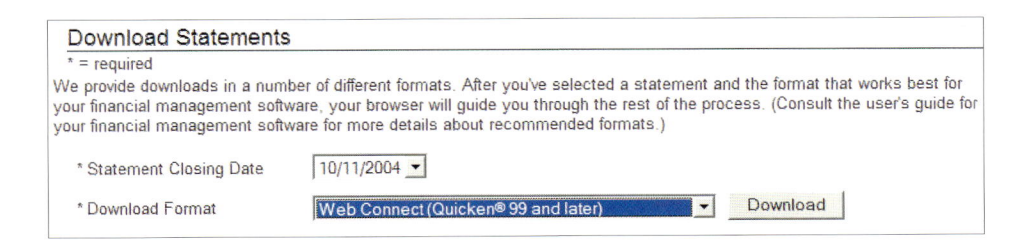

Quicken automatically imports the file, and the Online Update Summary window appears. Click the Go to Register button for the account you just downloaded.

The register appears, with the downloaded transactions in the bottom pane of the register. See the compare transactions section later in this chapter to learn how to deal with the downloaded transactions.

On the Mac, use your Web browser to log in to your financial institution's Web site. Navigate to where you can download your account statement, then follow the on-screen instructions to download the file. After the file has downloaded, Quicken will automatically launch and import the file (if you are using Safari or Internet Explorer). When Quicken is done with the downloaded transactions, the Online Transmission Summary appears. Click OK, and Quicken displays the Download Transactions window. See the compare transactions section to learn how to deal with the downloaded transactions.

compare transactions

After downloading banking transactions, Quicken compares those transactions to ones already in your account registers. Some downloaded transactions will match items that exist in the register, and Quicken labels these as Matched. Other transactions that aren't already in the register will be labeled as New. In either case, you may need to properly categorize the transaction, and then you accept the transaction into Quicken. Quicken will then mark all of the accepted transactions as cleared in your account register.

To compare, match, and accept downloaded transactions on Windows, begin by looking for the flagged accounts in the Account Bar. The flag signifies that you have downloaded transactions that need to be dealt with (a flag can also denote an account with scheduled transactions that are due).

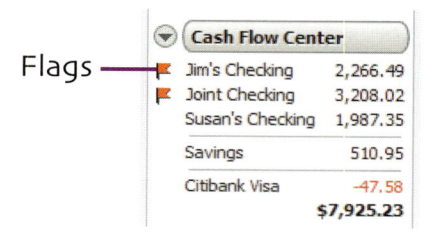

Flags

Click one of the flagged accounts in the Account Bar. The Transactions tab of the account will appear, split in two. The top pane is the account register, and the bottom pane contains the downloaded transactions.

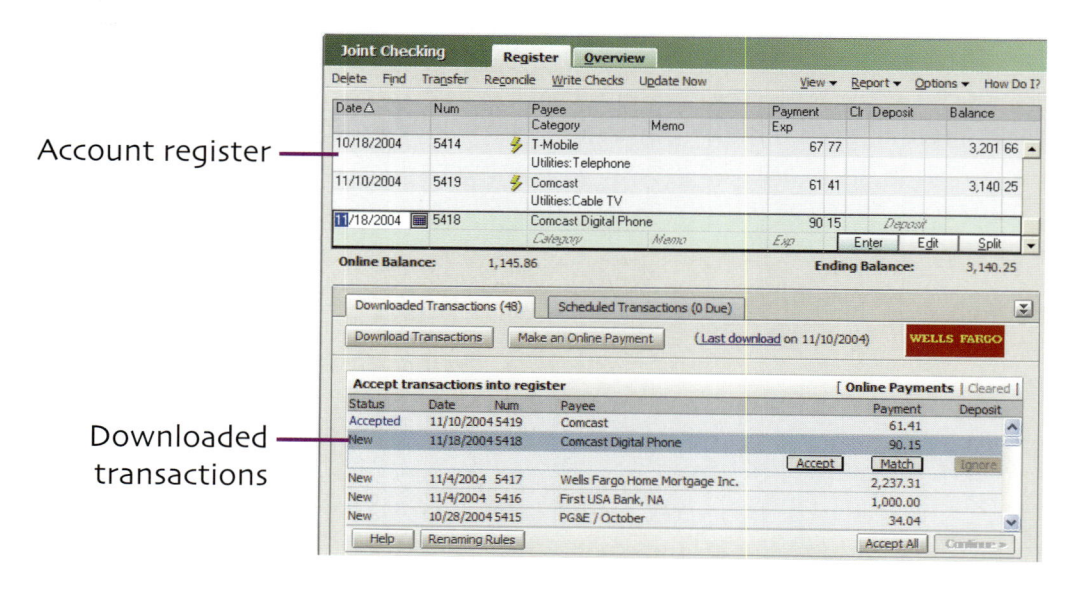

Account register

Downloaded transactions

bank and pay bills online

In the Accept transactions into register section, transactions that already exist in your account register will be labeled as Match in the Status column. Transactions not in your register will be labeled New.

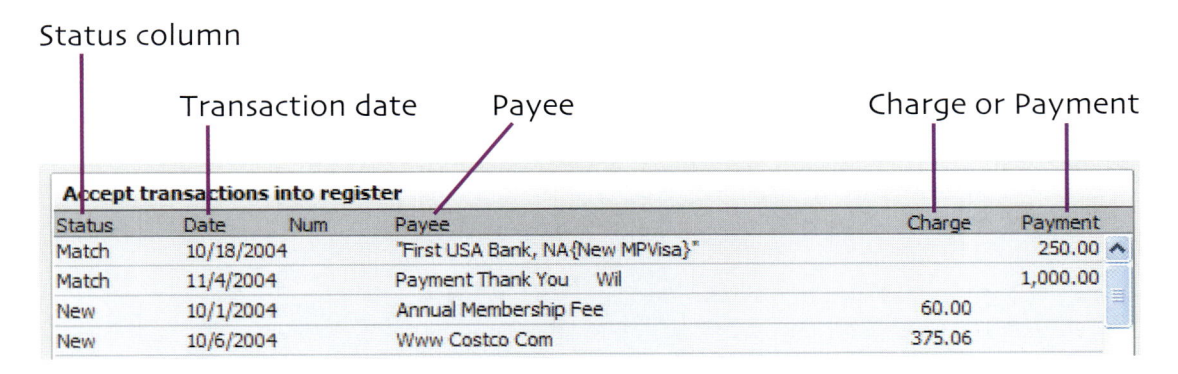

Status column

Transaction date   Payee   Charge or Payment

Accept transactions into register					
Status	Date	Num	Payee	Charge	Payment
Match	10/18/2004		"First USA Bank, NA{New MPVisa}"		250.00
Match	11/4/2004		Payment Thank You Wil		1,000.00
New	10/1/2004		Annual Membership Fee	60.00	
New	10/6/2004		Www Costco Com	375.06	

Click the first downloaded transaction. Two buttons, labeled Accept and Edit, will appear below the transaction.

Status	Date	Num	Payee	Charge	Payment
Match	10/18/2004		"First USA Bank, NA{New MPVisa}"		250.00
				Accept	Edit▼

bank and pay bills online

compare transactions

If it is a matched transaction, Quicken will highlight the transaction in the register in the top half of the window. Click Accept. The status for the transaction will change to Accepted.

If the transaction is labeled New, you may have to enter the payee or category of the transaction (Quicken will remember this category for subsequent similar transactions). Click to select the new transaction, and it will appear in the account register.

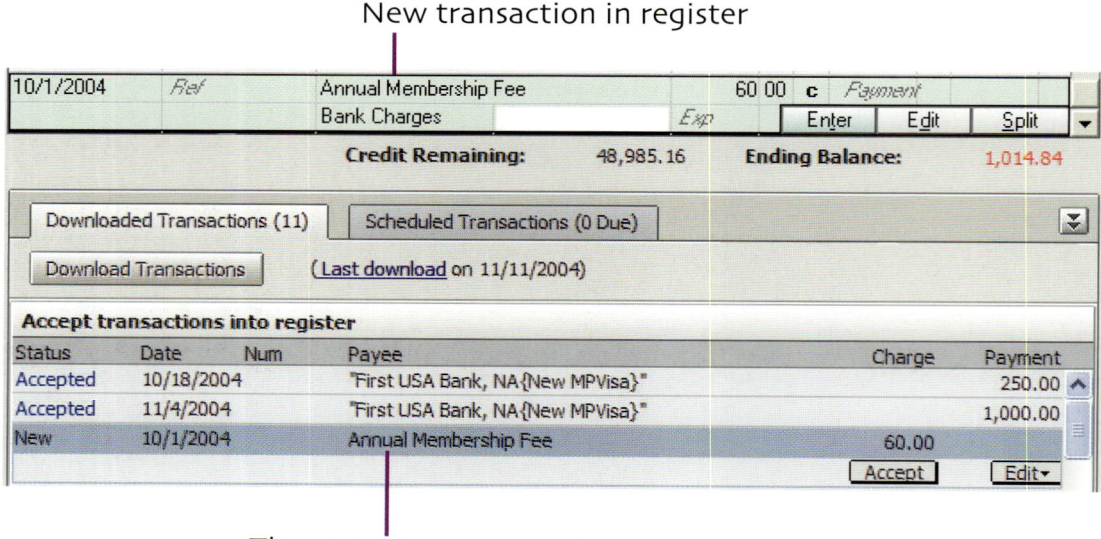

New transaction in register

The same new transaction in the downloaded transaction list

If necessary, categorize the transaction in the account register, then click Enter in the account register. The downloaded transaction will change to Accepted. Repeat matching and accepting transactions until all of them have been accepted, then click Done at the bottom of the Accept transactions into register section.

bank and pay bills online

On the Mac, after you have completed downloading transactions, the Download Transactions window appears. Because you could have downloaded transactions from multiple financial institutions, choose the one that you want from the Financial Institution pop-up menu. You may also have multiple accounts at the same financial institution, so choose the account that you want from the Account pop-up menu.

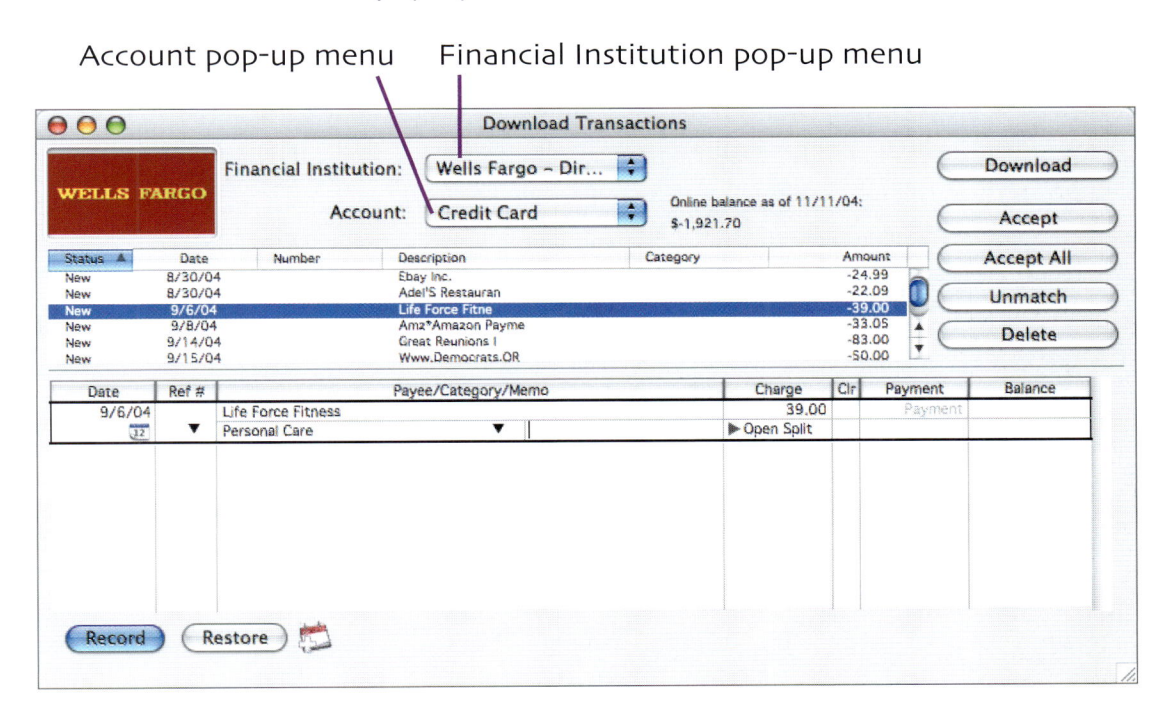

Account pop-up menu   Financial Institution pop-up menu

Quicken displays the downloaded transactions for the selected financial institution and account in the top half of the Download Transactions window. Quicken compares the downloaded transactions with transactions that are already in your account register. If the transactions correspond, the word Matched appears in the Status column, otherwise the word New appears. You will first convert all of the New transactions to Matched transactions, then you can accept them into your account register.

bank and pay bills online 71

compare transactions

Click to select the top New downloaded transaction. It will appear in the register in the bottom half of the window. If necessary, enter the payee or category of the transaction, then click the Record button at the bottom of the window. The transaction will change to Matched. Repeat this process for all of the New transactions.

New transaction in downloaded transaction list

New	9/15/04		Www.Democrats.OR			-50.00	
New	9/18/04		Merch Interest			-21.94	
New	9/17/04		Applebee'S Hop39			-51.53	
Date	Ref #		Payee/Category/Memo			Charge	Clr	Pay
8/7/04		Adel'S Restaurant				36.18	
		Dining					
9/6/04		Life Force Fitness				39.00	C
		Personal Care					
9/15/04		Www.Democrats.org				50.00	
		Political Contribution	▼	Memo		▶ Open Split	

New transaction in register after category added

After you have matched all the transactions, select each transaction and click the Accept button, or click Accept All. Quicken removes the accepted items from the transaction list in the Download Transactions window. Close the Download Transactions window by clicking its close box.

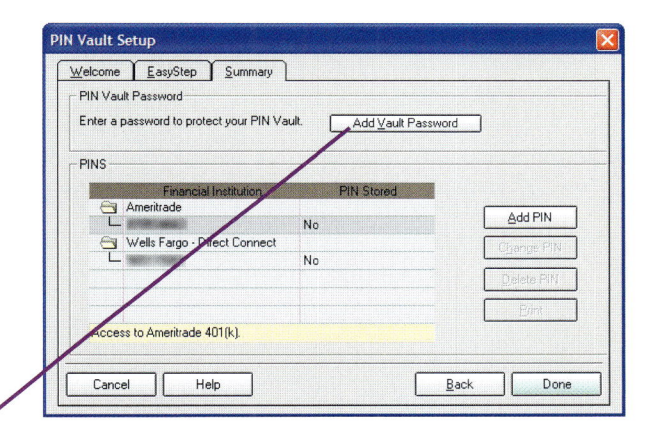

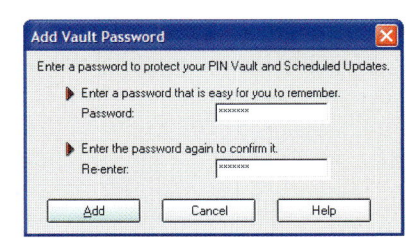

organize your pins (Win)

All of the online financial accounts that you use will require a PIN in order to access them. It's not a good idea to use the same PIN for all of your accounts, because you don't want a situation where someone learns the PIN for one of your accounts, and then has access to all of them. But it can be difficult to remember different PINs for many accounts. Quicken's PIN Vault consolidates all of the PINs for the online accounts you access through Quicken, allowing you to unlock all of the accounts by entering just one password.

To set up your PIN Vault on Windows, choose Online > PIN Vault > Set Up. The PIN Vault Setup dialog appears, set to the Welcome tab, which explains what the PIN Vault does. Click the Summary tab.

The first thing you need to do is to add the password that you will use to unlock the PIN Vault. Click Add Vault Password. In the resulting dialog, enter the password, then enter it again, and then click Add.

Next, you'll add the PINs for each account to the Vault. You'll only have to do this once. Click to select the account number of the first account, then click Add PIN. In the resulting dialog, enter the PIN twice, then click Add. Under the PIN Stored column of the PIN Vault Setup dialog, the status will change to Yes.

Continue adding PINs for each of the remaining accounts, then click Done.

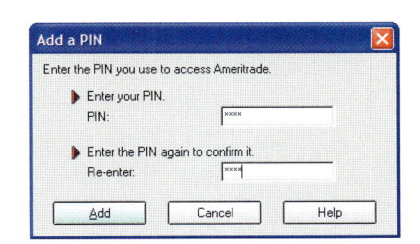

bank and pay bills online   **73**

organize your pins (Mac)

To set up your PIN Vault on the Mac, choose Online > PIN Vault. The Online Account Updates window appears, set to the PIN Vault tab. Click Create PIN Vault.

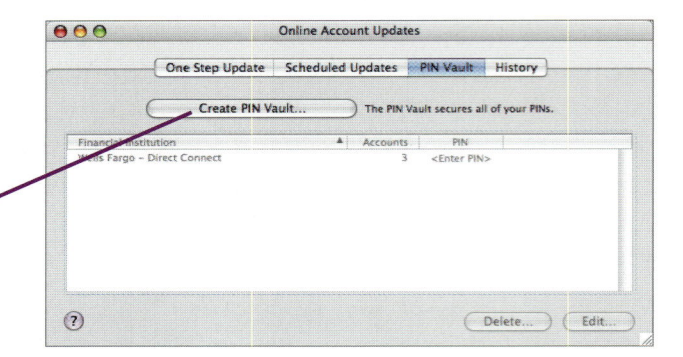

In the resulting dialog, enter the password you want to use, then enter it again, and then click OK.

To add the PINs for your accounts, click on the first account, and click Edit. The Enter PIN dialog appears. Enter the PIN as requested, then click OK.

Continue adding PINs for each of your remaining accounts, then close the Online Account Updates window by clicking its close box.

bank and pay bills online

use one step update

Quicken allows you to have many different online-enabled accounts, at different financial institutions. For example, you could have different checking accounts at different banks, plus one or more online brokerage accounts from which you can download your investment transactions. It wouldn't be convenient for you to have to check each one of these accounts separately, so Quicken's One Step Update feature allows you check all of your online accounts at once. Almost anything that you want to do online in Quicken, you can do with One Step Update, including download transactions from your banking, credit card, and investment accounts; update investment prices; pay bills; and upload financial information to Quicken.com so that you can view it wherever you are.

One Step Update uses the PIN Vault to store the different PINs for each account. The PIN Vault feeds your personal identification numbers to One Step Update as needed.

If your financial institution uses the Web Connect method to download transactions, you can't include that institution in your One Step Update. Instead, you must download transactions through the financial institution's Web site.

To start up a One Step Update on Windows, click the Update button on the Toolbar, or choose Online > One Step Update.

The One Step Update dialog appears. Click to select which items you want to include in the update, then click Update Now.

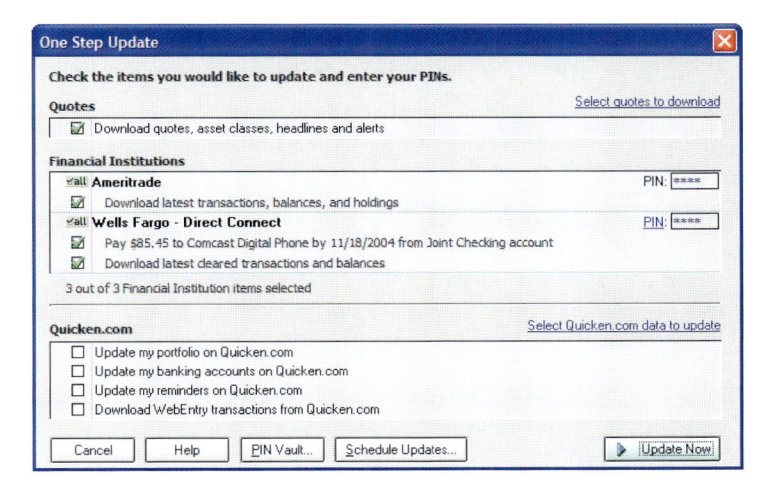

bank and pay bills online

use one step update (cont.)

Quicken will connect to your financial institutions, and will keep you apprised of its progress with the One Step Update Status dialog.

After the download is complete, the Online Update Summary window appears. If there are transactions that need to be reviewed, you can click the Go to Register button to go directly to that account's register. Otherwise, click Continue to close the window.

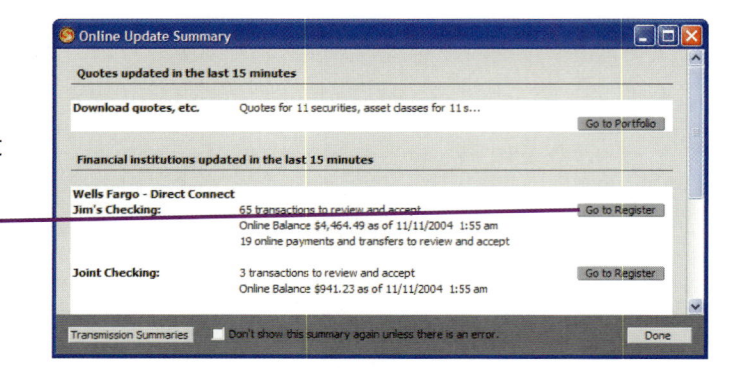

To start up a One Step Update on the Mac, click the One Step button on the Toolbar, or choose Online > One Step Update.

In the Online Account Updates window, choose the items that you wish to update, then click Update Now.

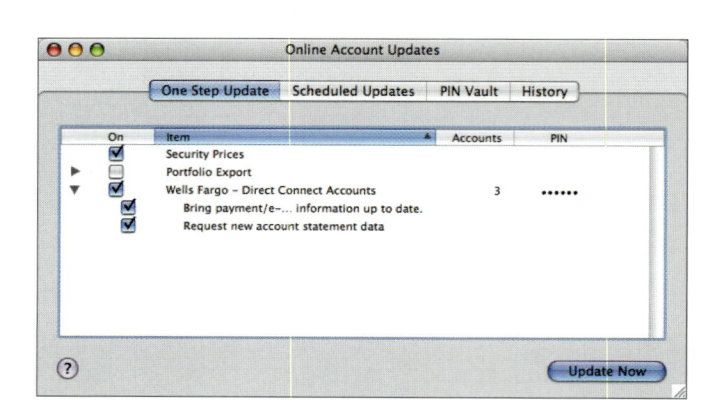

Quicken will connect to your financial institution. After the download is complete, the Online Transmission Summary Window will appear. Click OK. If transactions were downloaded from your financial institutions, the Download Transaction window will appear, allowing you to review and accept the transactions.

bank and pay bills online

create online payees

Making online payments with Quicken makes paying your bills extremely quick and convenient. You'll begin by setting up the payment recipients in the Online Payees list.

To create an online payee, choose Online > Online Payees List (Online > Payments > Online Payees). The Online Payees List opens. Click New.

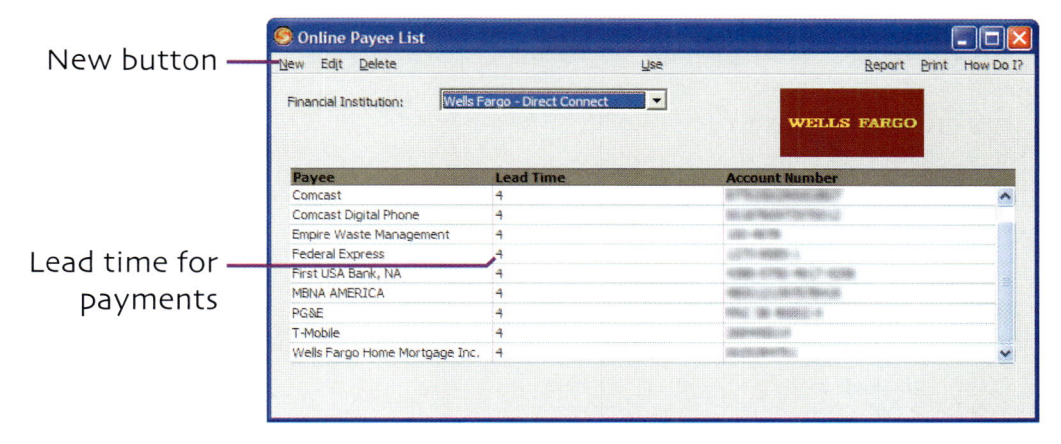

Online Payees List for Windows

Online Payees List for Mac

bank and pay bills online   77

create online payees

The Set Up Online Payee dialog appears. Enter the name of the online payee, the billing address, your account number with the payee, and the contact number of the payee. You can usually find all of this information on your billing statement. When you're done entering the information, click OK. A confirmation dialog will appear allowing you to check your work. Check it carefully, as you want to make sure that any payments you make are correctly credited to your account. Click Accept.

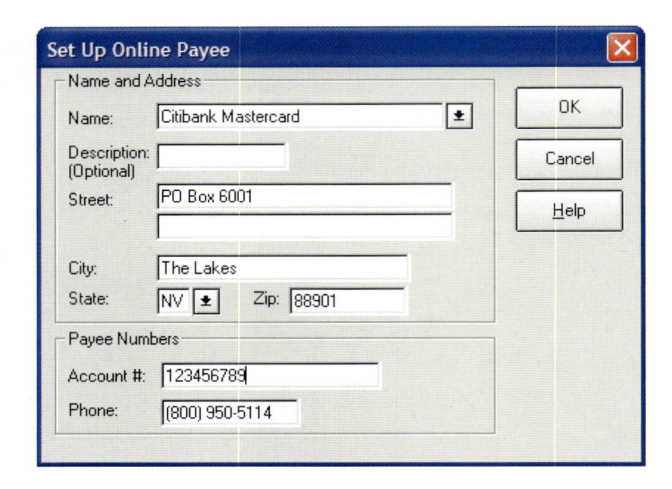

pay bills online

Paying bills online is a lot like entering any other payment in your checking account register, except that you don't have to actually write a paper check. Just enter the payment in Quicken and send it off.

Begin by opening the account register that you want to use to make the payment. Click in the blank transaction at the bottom of the register. Enter the date that you want the online payment to occur. This date can't be today's date; because it takes a few days to process the online payment, you must pick a future date. Different payees take different amounts of time to be paid, and your bank knows how long it takes for most payees. If you want to know how many days it takes for a payment to post, open the Online Payees List, and look at the Lead Time column. Press Tab.

In the Num field of the register, type S, which will bring up the pop-up menu set to Send Online Payment (on the Mac, it's just Send). Press the Tab key to get to the Payee field.

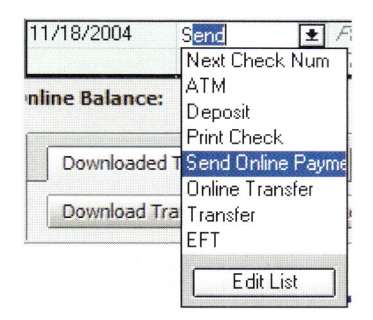

In the Payee field, begin typing the name of one of your online payees. Quicken's QuickFill feature will complete the name after a few letters. If you type a name that is not in the Online Payees List, it will walk you through the process of adding a new online payee. Enter the payment amount, category, and (optionally) a memo, then click Enter (Record). Repeat as needed to enter more payments.

To send your payments, do a One Step Update.

bank and pay bills online

transfer money online

If you have more than one online-enabled account at a particular financial institution, and if that institution allows you to transfer money online between those accounts, you can transfer the funds electronically through Quicken.

On Windows, click the Online Center button in the Toolbar or choose Online > Online Center..

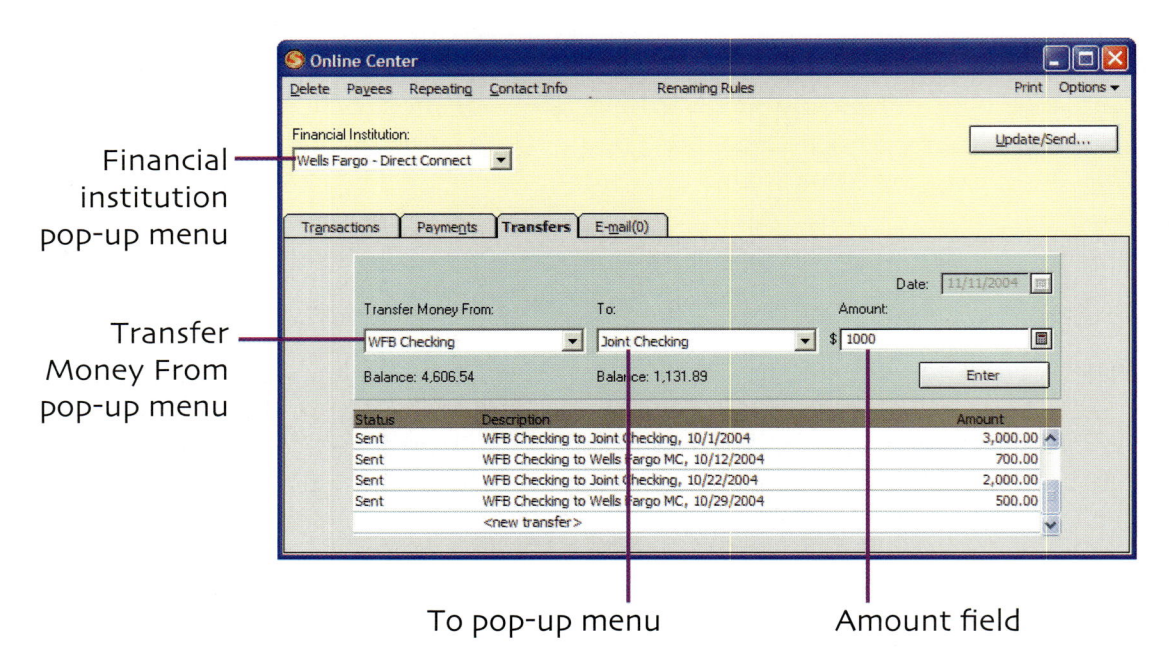

Financial institution pop-up menu

Transfer Money From pop-up menu

To pop-up menu   Amount field

Choose the financial institution you want from the Financial Institution pop-up menu. Choose the source of the funds from the Transfer Money From pop-up menu, and the destination of the funds from the To pop-up menu. Quicken shows you the balance of each account underneath the source and destination. Enter the transfer amount in the Amount field, then click the Enter button. To send the payment, click the Update/Send button.

The Online Center window appears. Click the Transfers tab.

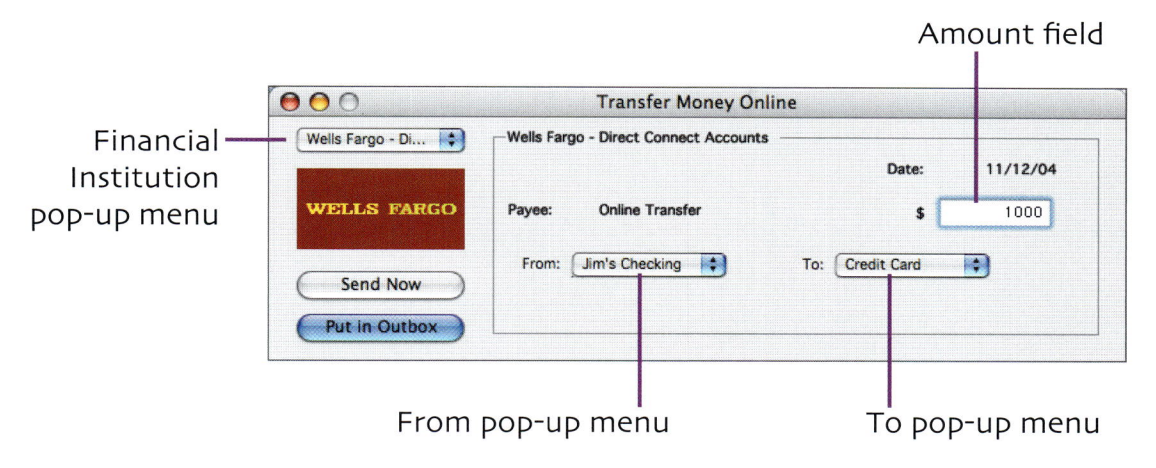

Amount field

Financial Institution pop-up menu

From pop-up menu

To pop-up menu

On the Mac, choose Online > Transfer Money Online.

In the resulting dialog, choose the financial institution you want from the Financial Institution pop-up menu. Enter the transfer amount in the Amount field. Choose the source of the funds from the From pop-up menu, and the destination of the funds from the To pop-up menu. To send the payment, click the Send Now button.

bank and pay bills online

extra bits

set up online accounts p. 62

- Even if your financial institution doesn't support online banking, you can still use online bill payment through Intuit, which allows you to pay anyone, regardless of whether they can accept online payments (if necessary, Intuit writes and mails a paper check for you).

- Each financial institution sets its own fees for online banking, and the amount varies from bank to bank, so it's a good idea to shop around for the best deal.

- There are approximately 2,000 financial institutions that support online access for Quicken for Windows, and about 1,300 that support online access for Quicken for Mac. You can get an up-to-date list of the financial institutions by choosing Online > Participating Financial Institutions on Windows or by choosing Online > Financial Institutions on the Mac, then clicking the Update List button.

- Depending on your financial institution, you'll connect and download transactions in one of two fashions. The first, Direct Connect, is the easiest and best way to connect. It allows Quicken to connect directly with your bank's computers to download transactions, exchange payment instructions, transfer funds between accounts, and exchange e-mail about your accounts. Financial institutions that don't support Direct Connect instead offer Web Connect, which uses the bank's Web site in conjunction with your Web browser to do some of the work of displaying and downloading your financial information. Financial institutions that use Web Connect require you to go to the bank's Web site and log in before you can download your account transactions. Web Connect downloads a file with the transactions to your computer; Quicken then reads the file and imports the transactions.

- Worried about the security of online banking? Don't be. Besides the security provided by your PINs, Quicken encrypts all of the information that is transferred back and forth. Encryption is a technique that scrambles data before it is sent using a mathematical algorithm. At the other end, your bank unscrambles the data. Quicken uses 128-bit DES (Data Encryption Standard) encryption along with SSL (Secure Sockets Layer) transfer protocols. This makes online banking through Quicken even more secure than, for example, purchasing goods and services from online merchants.

compare transactions p. 68

- Your financial institution may label ATM transactions and service charges as EFT, which stands for Electronic Funds Transfer.
- If you turn on Auto-Reconcile, Quicken will automatically begin the reconciliation process after you complete comparing transactions. See the Quicken User Guide for information about turning on Auto-Reconcile.

organize your pins p. 73

- Make the password that you use to lock up the PIN Vault different from any of the PINs that are stored in the Vault. That way if the password for the Vault is compromised, you haven't given away the keys for any of the individual accounts.
- When you pick a PIN, don't use easy to figure out numbers such as the numeric portion of your street address, or your birthday, or the last four digits of your telephone number. The whole point of a PIN is security. Instead, use combinations of numbers that you don't have trouble remembering but that other people wouldn't know or couldn't easily find out, like the number of your college dorm room.
- Once your PINs are in the PIN Vault, you cannot view them within Quicken, because they appear as asterisks in the program. But on Quicken for Windows, you can print a listing of them, revealing each PIN. Choose Online > PIN Vault > Edit. You'll be asked for your PIN Vault password. Enter the password, then in the PIN Vault dialog, click the Print button.

bank and pay bills online

extra bits

pay bills online p. 79

- If your payee is set up to receive electronic funds transfers, payment is transferred directly from your account to your payee's account. This takes between two and four business days. If the payee doesn't accept EFTs, your financial institution prints a paper check and sends it to the payee by U.S. mail. It's important that you allow sufficient time for the payment to get to the payee to avoid a late charge, so make sure that you schedule payments at least three or four days before a payment due date.

- Don't forget that a payee will often need a day or two after receiving a check to process the payment and credit your account.

transfer money online p. 80

- Money transferred between online accounts will usually be transferred between those accounts on the next business day.

- Transfers and credit card accounts are dealt with as payments, and transfers from credit card accounts to checking or savings accounts are usually considered to be cash advances. You should check with your bank for their detailed policy on such transfers, since fees may apply.

6. balance your accounts

Balancing your checkbook by hand is a pain, especially if you have slacked off for a few months and need to catch up. It's even worse if you've never been in the habit of balancing your checkbook. I know this, because I used to be one of those people. For me, one of the biggest benefits of using Quicken to balance my checkbook was that a chore that often took an hour to do by hand became easy to do in just a few minutes. If you use online banking and turn on Quicken's Auto-Reconcile feature, it can even do the account balancing for you.

Quicken isn't limited to just reconciling your checkbook, however. You can also balance your savings and credit card accounts. In this chapter, you'll learn how to reconcile accounts and resolve any differences between the bank's records and your own.

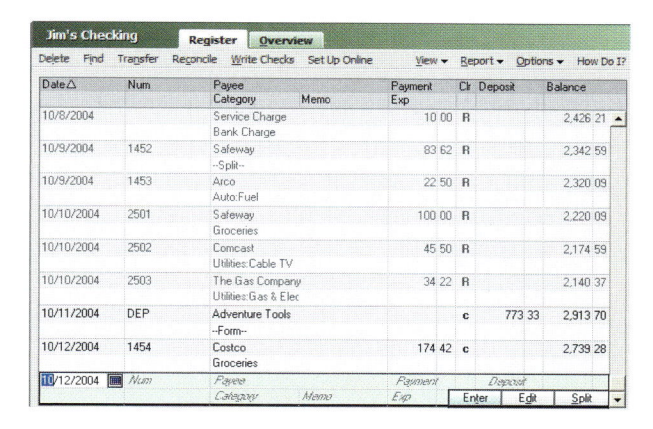

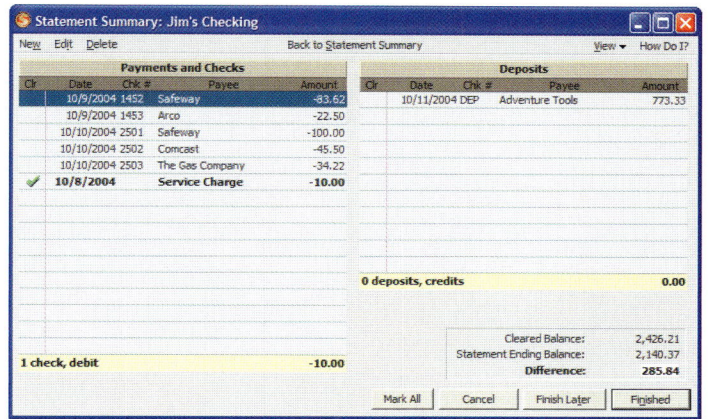

balance accounts

You'll use the same procedure to balance a checking, savings, money market, or credit card account. You'll need your bank or credit card statement. First, you enter your statement closing balance, and then you match transactions on your statement with transactions in your Quicken account register.

Before you begin, you should make sure that you have entered into Quicken all transactions that occurred between the date of your last statement and the date of your current statement. If you need to reconcile for more than one month, you first need to reconcile your account with the bank statements for each of the prior months before you try to reconcile the current month's statement.

To get started, open the register for the account you want to balance, then choose Cash Flow > Reconcile (Activities > Reconcile). The Statement Summary (on the Mac it's called Reconcile Startup) dialog appears. The Opening Balance field will be filled in (with the ending balance from the last time that you reconciled; if you have never reconciled before, you may have to go back and reconcile a prior month).

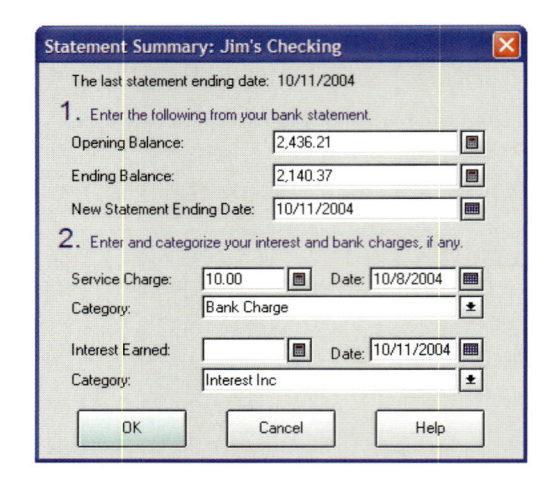

In the Ending Balance field, enter the ending balance from your bank statement, and enter your statement closing date in the New Statement Ending Date field. If the account has a service charge associated with it, enter it in the Service Charge field, and enter the date the charge was applied to your account (often it's the same date as the statement closing date). If necessary, choose the Category for the service charge. If the account earns interest, enter the amount, date, and category of the interest payment. Click OK. The Reconcile dialog opens.

balance your accounts

Any service charges or interest payments will show up in the Payments and Checks section already cleared. Compare your bank statement with the transactions shown, and click on each transaction that matches. As you clear each transaction, a check mark appears next to it in the Clr column.

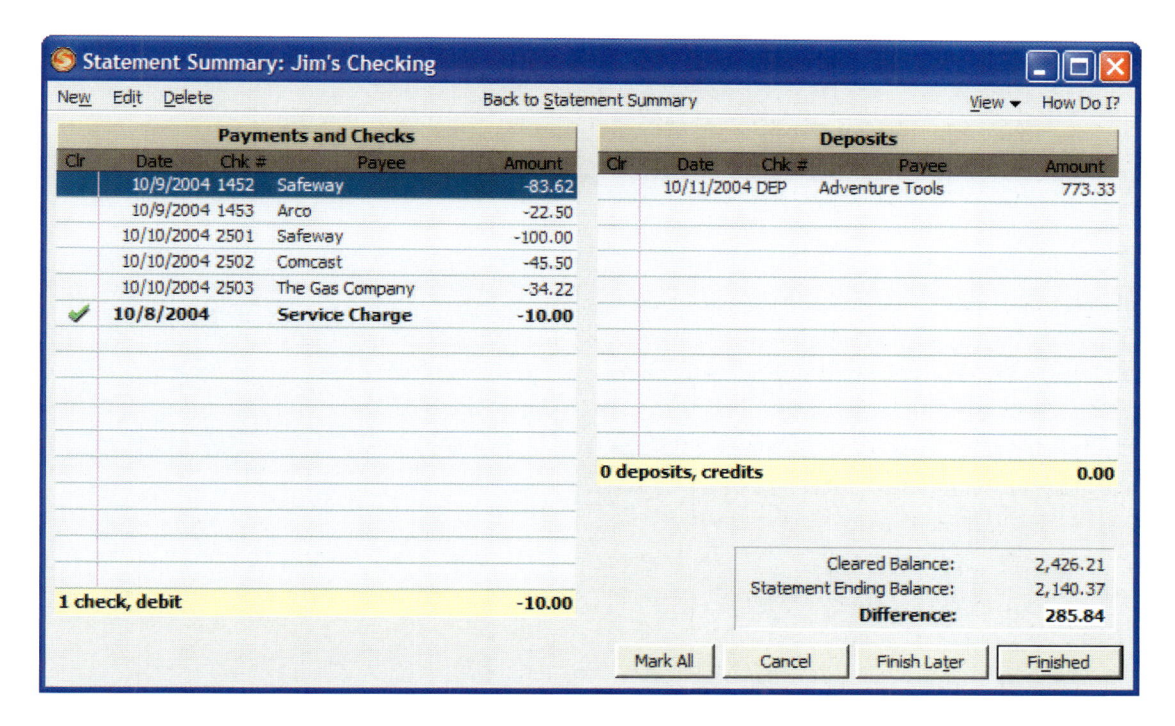

Statement Summary: Jim's Checking							
New Edit Delete			Back to Statement Summary			View ▼	How Do I?
Payments and Checks				**Deposits**			
Clr	Date	Chk #	Payee	Amount	Clr	Date	Chk #	Payee	Amount
	10/9/2004	1452	Safeway	-83.62		10/11/2004	DEP	Adventure Tools	773.33
	10/9/2004	1453	Arco	-22.50					
	10/10/2004	2501	Safeway	-100.00					
	10/10/2004	2502	Comcast	-45.50					
	10/10/2004	2503	The Gas Company	-34.22					
✓	10/8/2004		Service Charge	-10.00					

0 deposits, credits   0.00

1 check, debit   -10.00

Cleared Balance: 2,426.21
Statement Ending Balance: 2,140.37
Difference: 285.84

[Mark All] [Cancel] [Finish Later] [Finished]

If you need to change a transaction (perhaps because you originally entered it incorrectly in the register), double-click the transaction in the Reconcile dialog to open the account register and edit it. To add a missing transaction, click the New (New Transaction) button in the Reconcile dialog to open the account register and make the addition.

balance your accounts

balance accounts (cont.)

As you check off each transaction, Quicken updates the Difference figure in the lower-right corner of the dialog. Once you check off all the transactions, that figure should be zero. If it is, click the Finished (Finish) button.

If the Difference amount is not zero after checking off all transactions, skip to correct differences on the next page to find out how to correct the problem.

If you balance successfully, the Reconciliation Complete dialog appears. On Windows, if you want to create a reconciliation report (you usually will not), click Yes. Otherwise, click No. In the account register, the transactions you checked off will be marked with an R in the Clr column.

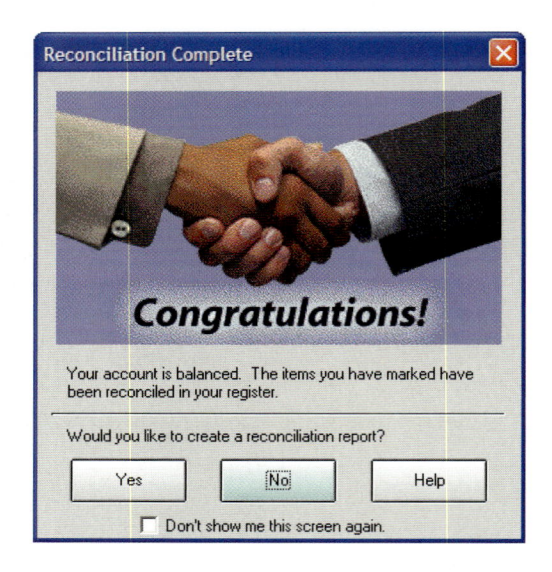

balance your accounts

correct differences

In the Reconcile dialog, if the Difference amount is not zero, it means that your account is not balancing for the current statement period. This usually occurs for one of two reasons: either a wrong number of payment or deposit items have been checked or some of the checked items have incorrect dollar amounts.

First you have to find the mistake. Begin by counting the number of credit items on your bank statement, and then count the number of deposits shown in the Reconcile dialog. If the number doesn't match, you've found the problem. Either add the deposit you forgot to enter into Quicken using the New (New Transaction) button, or uncheck a deposit that you marked in error.

If the problem isn't with credits, it is with the checks and payments. Compare the number of checks and payments on your bank statement against the number of debit items in the Reconcile dialog. It's possible that you may not have recorded an item in the register, or you might have duplicated a transaction, entered a payment as a deposit or a deposit as a payment, or marked an item cleared by mistake. You may have also missed adding bank service charges to your register that you'll find on your statement.

If the number of items is correct but the statement still doesn't balance, you have a problem with the dollar amount of one or more of your items. By hand or using a calculator, add up all the transactions shown under Payments and Checks, and compare the total with the total of debits on the statement. If the numbers don't match, you have a problem with the dollar amount of one or more of the debits. Compare each transaction on the statement with the corresponding entry under Payments and Checks until you find the culprit. If the debits are okay, check the dollar amounts of all the Deposits.

correct differences (cont.)

If the dollar amount of an unreconciled balance is small, you may decide that it's not worth the time it takes to track down the mistake. In that case, you can let Quicken enter a register adjustment, which will force your account to reconcile. If you click the Finished button in the Reconcile dialog while there is still a difference, Quicken will pop up the Adjust Balance dialog.

If you want Quicken to enter an account adjustment, click the Adjust button. If you want to take another whack at finding the mistake, click the Cancel button.

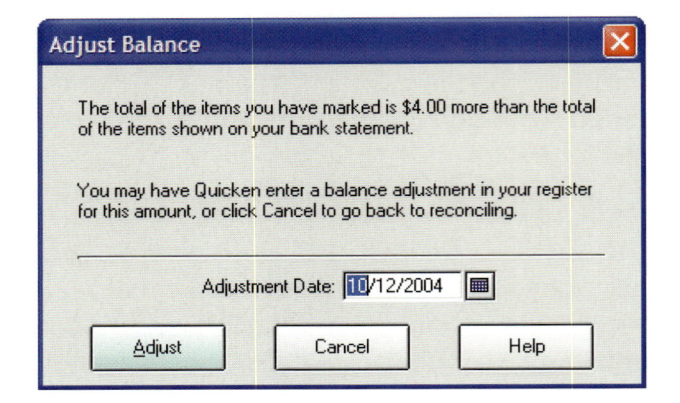

extra bits

balance accounts p. 86

- If you use online banking, Quicken's Auto-Reconcile can balance your accounts automatically, every time that you download transactions from your financial institutions. This saves you even more time. To turn on Auto-Reconcile on Windows on an account that has already been activated for online banking (see Chapter 5), choose Cash Flow > Reconcile. The Reconcile Online Account dialog opens. Make sure that Online Balance is selected, then check Auto reconcile after compare to register, then click OK. On the Mac, choose Quicken 2005 > Preferences, then click the Auto-Reconcile category. Check Enable Auto-Reconcile, then click OK.

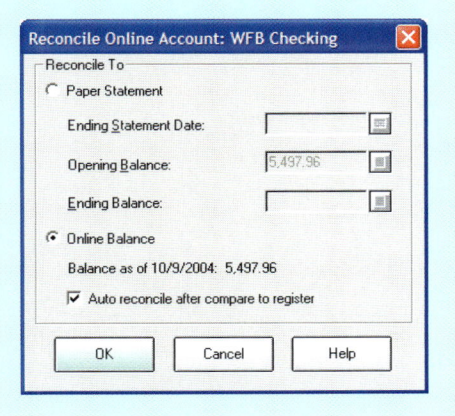

correct differences p. 89

- The most common mistake you'll find in your registers is transposing two digits in data entry.
- If you're off by a small amount that is a round number, it's likely that you missed a bank service charge. Check your statement carefully for charges you don't normally see, such as those for check printing or using another bank's ATM.
- Using online banking makes balancing your checkbook and other accounts even easier, because you download your bank and credit card statement directly into Quicken's account registers. This eliminates most data entry errors.

balance your accounts

7. manage your credit cards and mortgage

The most common forms of debt that people have are credit cards and the mortgage on their home. Naturally, Quicken can track both of these. Of the two, keeping on top of credit card debt is a key concern for many families. As purchases and interest charges mount, it's all too easy to get to the point where credit card debt becomes overwhelming.

One way to make sure that your credit card debt doesn't spin out of control is to track it carefully on a monthly basis. That means categorizing your card charges so that you know where you're spending your money and reconciling your credit card accounts to make sure that spending doesn't slip by unnoticed. In Chapter 8, you'll see how you can use Quicken's reports and graphs to get an even better view of your credit card spending.

For your home mortgage, you'll want to set up two accounts in Quicken: one showing the asset (your home's value) and the other tracking the liability (the mortgage on your home).

In this chapter, you'll learn how to use Quicken to manage your short-term debt such as credit cards, as well as keep track of your long-term debt, such as your mortgage.

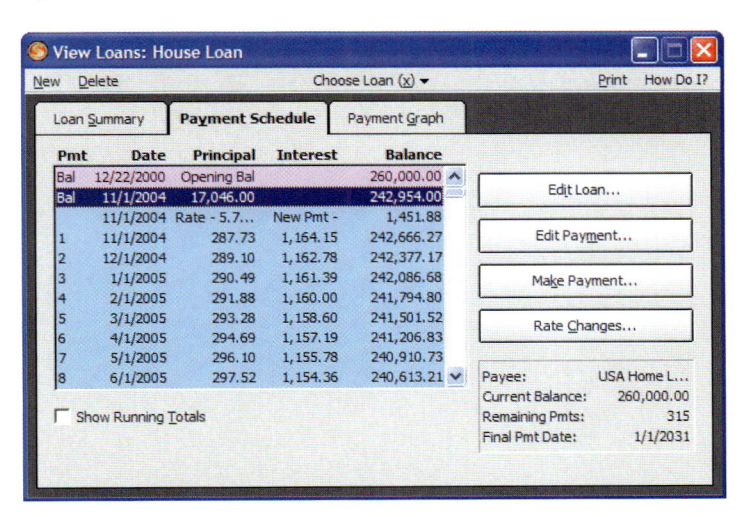

enter card charges

The best way to handle your credit cards in Quicken is to create a different account for each credit card. You'll enter each transaction into the account register, and you'll be able to see the current balance and reconcile the account with your credit card statement.

First, you'll need to create a credit card account for each of the credit cards that you want to track. See Chapter 2 if you need help creating the accounts.

Once you have your credit card accounts set up, you can enter transactions from your paper statement. Display the credit card account register by clicking the account in the Account Bar (Windows) or by choosing Lists > Registers > [Credit card account name] (Mac).

10/11/2004		Dem Sen Cmp Cmm		51 00	R		1,593 08
		Political Contribution					
10/11/2004		Dccc Internet		50 00	R		1,643 08
		Political Contribution					
10/14/2004	Ref	Payee		Charge		Payment	
		Category	Memo	Exp	Enter	Edit	Split

Enter the date, then press the Tab key to get to the Payee field (the Ref # field is usually not used; you might see something in it if you download your credit card statement). Enter the payee. Next, enter the charge amount.

Assign a category to the transaction by typing it into the Category field. Optionally, enter a memo about the transaction. Click Enter (Record).

make card payments

You usually don't need to enter payments to the credit card in the credit card register. When you make a payment to the credit card from your checking account, you will use a transfer category in the checking account register to show that money has flowed from the checking account to the credit card account, thereby decreasing the balance of the credit card account. Quicken automatically makes a corresponding entry in the credit card account. If you need more information about transfer categories, see transfer money in Chapter 4.

This $200 payment in the checking account register uses a transfer category for the destination of the transfer (the credit card account), which you can recognize because it is surrounded by square brackets ([ ]).

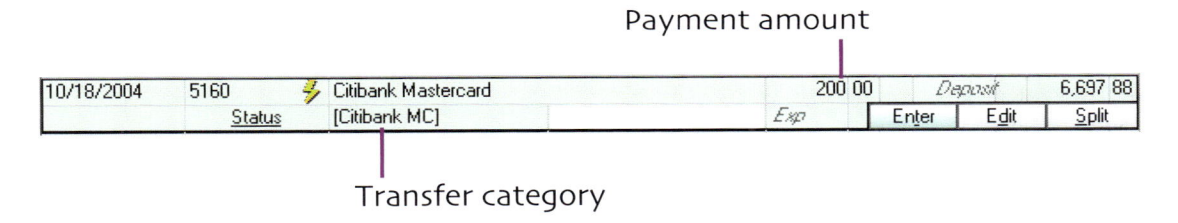

Payment amount

10/18/2004	5160		Citibank Mastercard		200 00	Deposit		6,697 88
	Status		[Citibank MC]		Exp	Enter	Edit	Split

Transfer category

The automatic entry made in the credit card account shows the payment. The category field in the credit card account shows the transfer category for the account the payment came from, in this case the checking account.

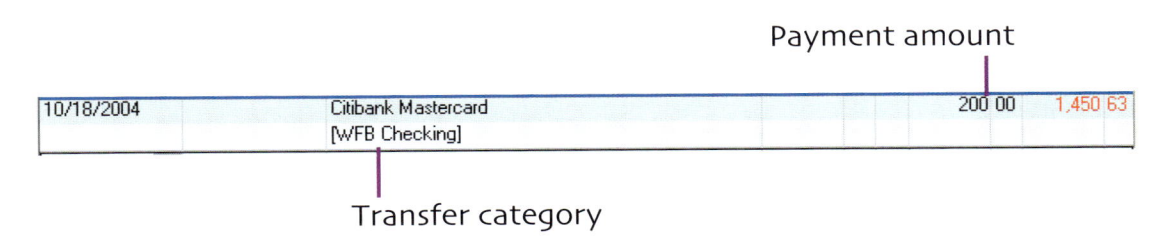

Payment amount

10/18/2004	Citibank Mastercard		200 00	1,450 63
	[WFB Checking]			

Transfer category

manage your credit cards and mortgage

mortgage setup (Win)

When you set up a loan for money you are borrowing, such as the money you've borrowed for your home mortgage, Quicken sets up two accounts. The asset account tracks the value of your home. The liability account tracks the balance and payments of the mortgage. As you make loan payments, Quicken keeps track of the balance of the loan's principal, and of how much you have paid in interest. This last number is especially important, because interest on home loans is tax-deductible.

Quicken for Windows uses an assistant to help you set up your loan and asset accounts. Begin by choosing Property & Debt > Property & Debt Accounts > Add Account. The Quicken Account Setup Assistant appears, with a choice of different loan types. Click House (with or without Mortgage), then click Next.

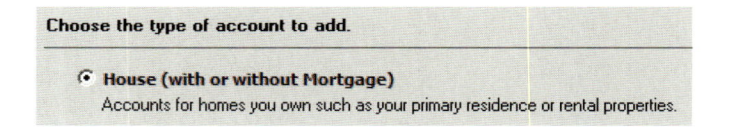

Give the account a name. This is the asset account, so you can use the choice that Quicken gives you (House), or you can use another descriptive name. Click Next. On the next screen, enter the date you bought the property, the purchase price you paid, and the current estimated value. You don't have to enter exact numbers here; you can change them later if needed. Click Next.

If there is a mortgage on the property, click Yes to create a liability account, then click Next.

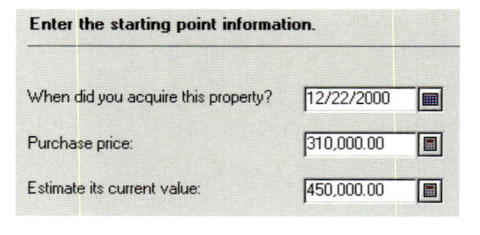

96   **manage your credit cards and mortgage**

The Edit Loan window appears, with the Opening Date already filled in (it is the same as the date you bought the property). Fill in the Opening Balance, the Original Length of the loan (typically 30 years for a home loan), the Compounding Period (that is how often interest is calculated; ask your lender if you're not sure), and how often you make payments. Click Next.

If you have a balloon payment, enter its information. Otherwise, from your latest mortgage statement, enter the loan's Current Balance and the as of date, the Payment Amount (add together both the Principal and Interest), the next payment date where it says due on, and the loan's Interest Rate. Click Done.

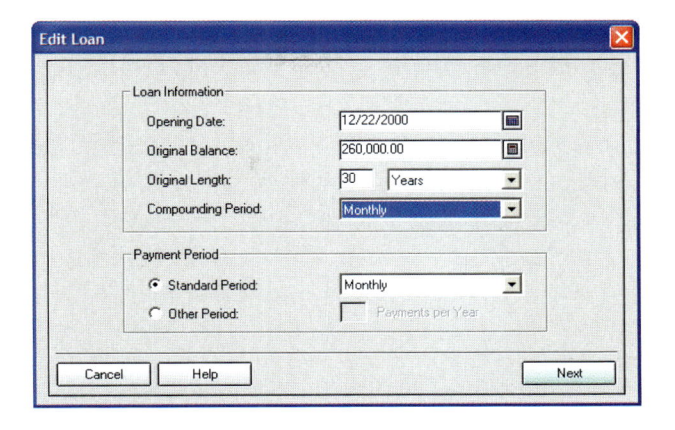

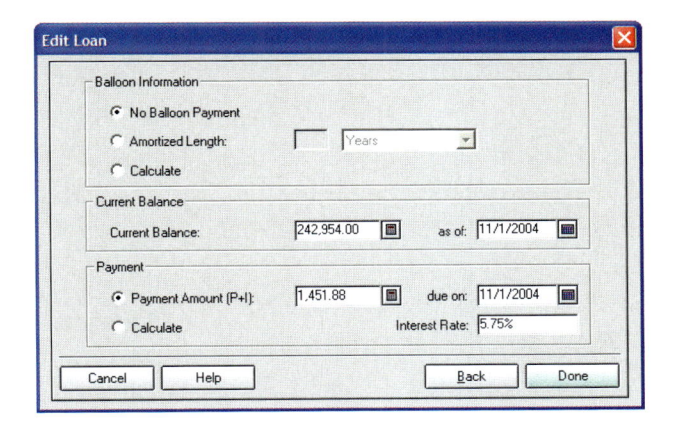

manage your credit cards and mortgage

mortgage setup (Win)

The Edit Loan Payment window appears. In the Payment section, the Current Interest Rate and Principal and Interest fields will already be filled in. If you have other amounts in your monthly payment—for example, if you make monthly contributions to an escrow account for property taxes—click the Edit button. A Split Transaction window will appear. Enter as many line items as you need to account for the extra monthly amounts you pay, then click OK. You'll return to the Edit Loan Payment window, and the total of the line items you added in the Split Transaction window appears in the Other amounts in payment field. Quicken calculates the Full Payment amount.

In the Transaction section, choose the payment Type (Payment or Print Check), and enter the Payee. Check that the Next Payment Date and Category for Interest are correct, then click OK.

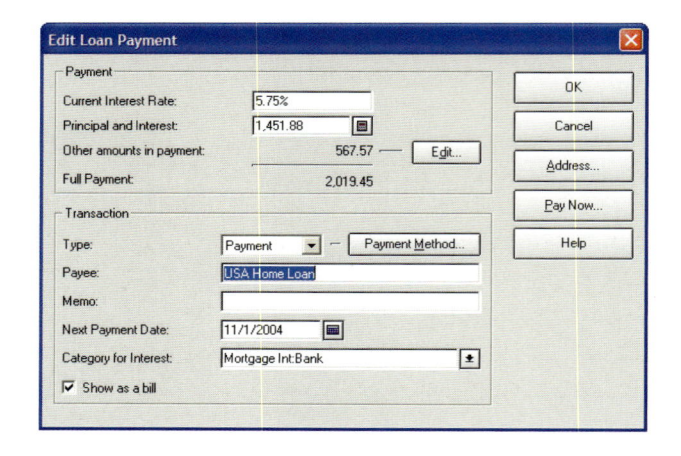

In the Account Bar, you can see that the asset (House) and liability (House Loan) accounts have been created. The asset account shows the current value of your home. The liability account, which is a negative number, shows how much you currently owe on your mortgage, and the total shows your home equity.

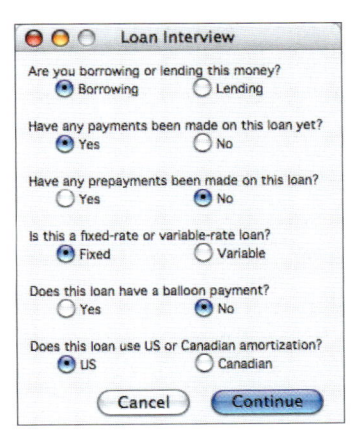

mortgage setup (Mac)

To set up your mortgage account, Quicken needs information about the terms of the loan and the lender. Then Quicken creates the loan payment schedule and liability account. As you make loan payments, Quicken keeps track of the balance of the loan's principal, and of how much you have paid in interest.

On the Mac, Quicken steps you through creating a loan with an assistant. Begin by choosing Lists > Loans. The Loans window appears.

Click the New button. The Loan Interview dialog appears.

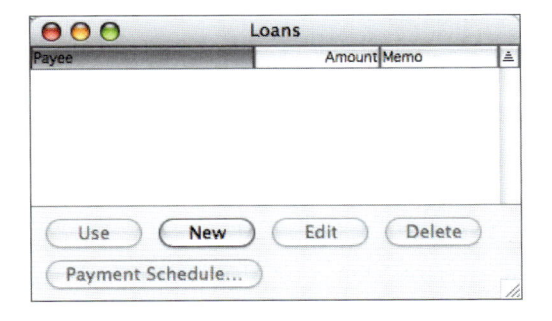

Select the radio buttons in the Loan Interview dialog that are appropriate for the loan you're creating, then click Continue. A second Loan Interview dialog appears, asking if you want to set up the loan beginning with the first payment or with the next payment due. I suggest that you start with the first payment. You'll need to know your payment amount, the original amount of the loan, the date that you made the first payment, the total number of payments, and the annual interest rate. Click First, and then click Continue.

manage your credit cards and mortgage   99

mortgage setup (Mac)

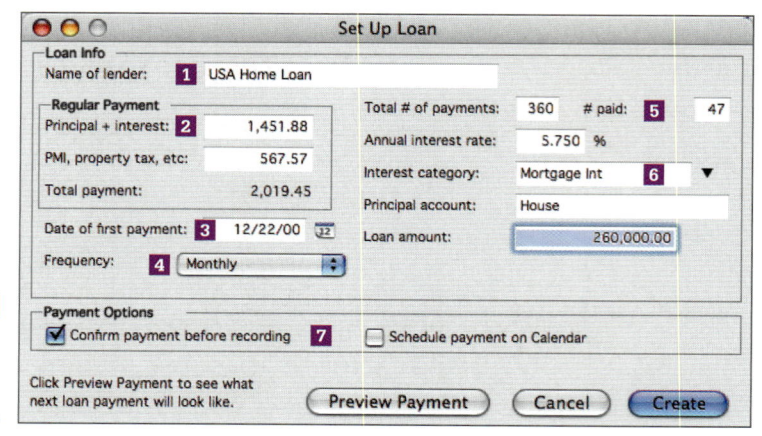

1 In the resulting Set Up Loan dialog, enter the name of your lender.

2 Enter the payment amounts. Enter the amount of your regular payment in the Principal + interest field. If you have one or more other amounts in your monthly payment—for example, if you make monthly contributions to an escrow account for property taxes—enter it in the PMI, property tax, etc. field.

3 Enter the date of your first payment.

4 Choose the frequency of the payment from the pop-up menu. Monthly is the default choice; change it if necessary.

5 Enter the Total # of payments. For example, for a 30-year mortgage, you'll have 360 payments. Quicken will calculate the number of payments that you have made since the first payment.

6 Enter the Annual interest rate, the interest expense category, and enter a name for the principal liability account that you'll use to track this loan. Quicken pops up a dialog confirming that you want to create a new liability account linked to this loan. Click Yes. Enter the beginning loan amount in the Loan amount field.

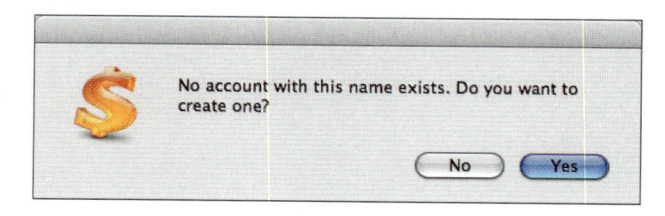

100   **manage your credit cards and mortgage**

7 If you want to be automatically reminded about your loan payment, check Schedule payment on Calendar in the Payment Options section.

8 To make sure that everything looks good before you finish creating the loan, click the Preview Payment button to open the Preview Payment dialog. If the loan information looks good, click OK to return to the Set Up Loan dialog.

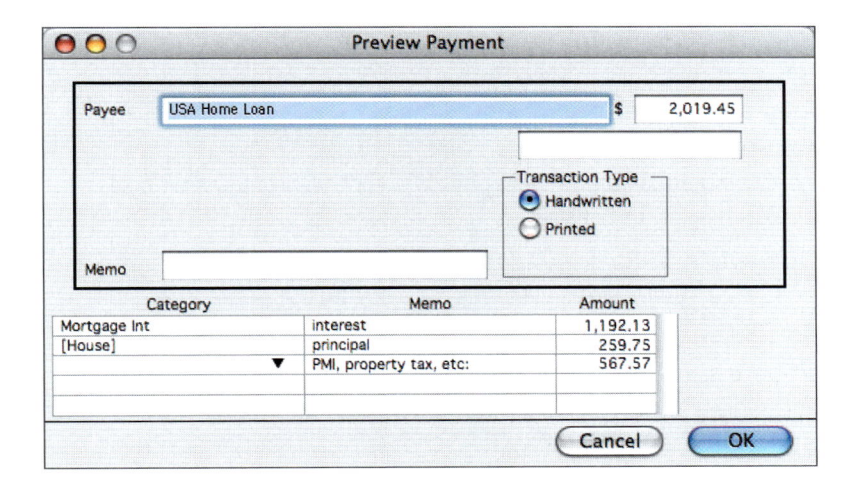

9 Click Create to save the loan information. The loan will appear in the Loans window.

make loan payments

To make a loan payment, you'll use the Loans window in Quicken for either Windows or Mac. The Loans window helps you make payments, and if you want to make an extra payment (such as an extra payment to go towards the loan's principal balance), you can do that, too.

On Windows, choose Property & Debt > Loans. The View Loans window appears.

The loan details are in the Loan Summary tab of the View Loans window. If you have more than one loan, you can switch between them with the Choose Loan menu at the top of the window.

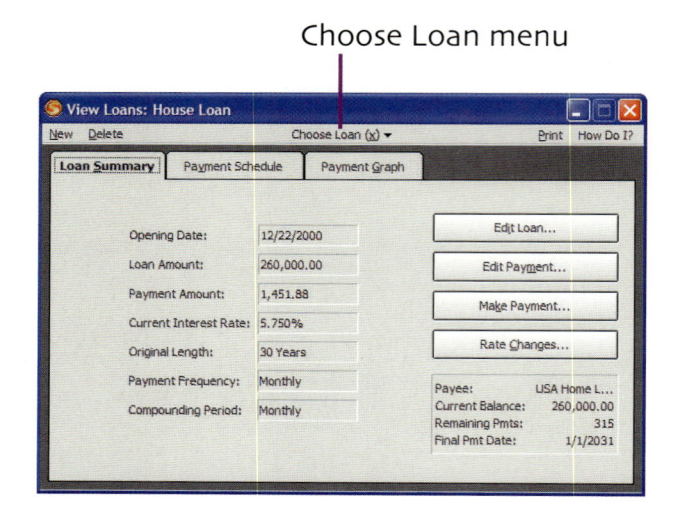

Click the Make Payment button. Quicken asks if this is a regular payment, or an extra payment. Click Regular or Extra.

manage your credit cards and mortgage

Depending on which button you clicked, the Make Regular Payment or Make Extra Payment dialog appears. Aside from the name, the dialogs are identical, except that the regular payment amount is already filled in, and you must fill in the amount of an extra payment. Choose the account from which you want to make the payment from the Account to use pop-up menu, review the other information in the window, and click OK to record the payment.

On the Mac, open the account register for the bank account from which you will make the loan payment. Choose Lists > Loans. The Loans window appears.

Select the loan for which you want to enter a payment and click the Use button, or simply double-click the loan's name. The Payment dialog appears.

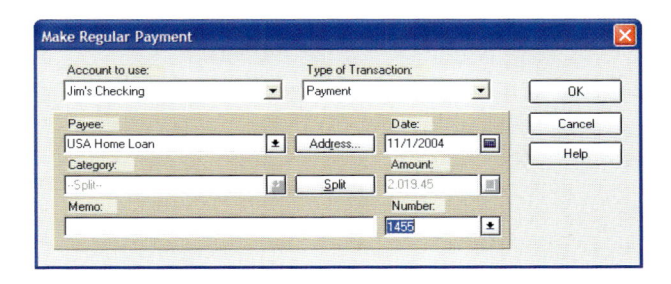

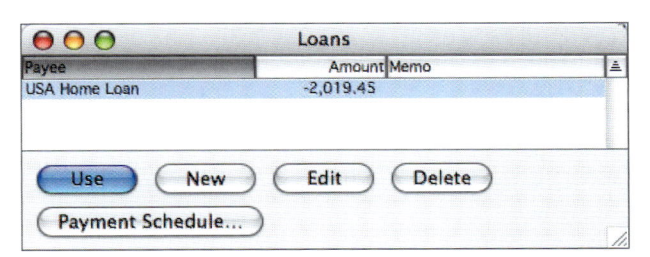

Enter any adjustments needed in the Payment dialog, then click OK. Quicken will enter the loan payment in the account register.

manage your credit cards and mortgage

track your mortgage

Quicken automatically calculates the payment schedule for the mortgage, detailing the date, payment number, principal amount, interest amount, and running balance until the end of the loan.

To view the payment schedule on Windows, choose Property & Debt > Loans to open the View Loans window. If you have more than one loan, choose the one you want with the Choose Loan menu at the top of the window. Then click the Payment Schedule tab.

On the Mac, choose Lists > Loans to open the Loans window. Click to select the loan you want to view, and then click the Payment Schedule button. The payment schedule window appears.

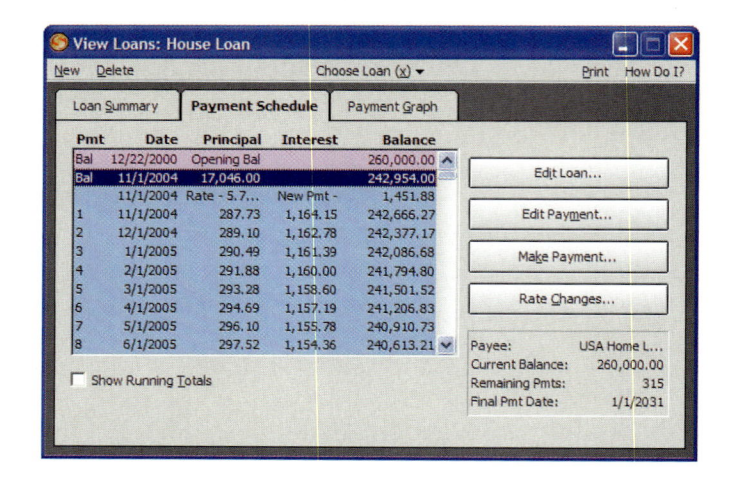

extra bits

enter card charges p. 94

- You can save yourself virtually all of the data entry associated with a credit card account by enabling online access and downloading your credit card statement over the Internet. In almost all cases, you can download each month's statement from the credit card provider's web site. You can then reconcile the account without needing to refer to paper statements at all, and if you have signed up for online banking, you can send your credit card payments electronically. This is absolutely the best and easiest way to deal with your credit cards; I haven't written a paper check for a credit card payment in years.

- If you have credit cards that you use infrequently, it may not be worth even the minor trouble of setting them up in Quicken. For example, I have an old department store credit card that I rarely use. On those occasions when I do use it, I pay off the card's balance with a check or online payment from my checking account, and categorize that payment in the checking account register with the appropriate category for the purchase.

make card payments p. 95

- If you won't be paying off your credit card balance in full every month, consider adding a scheduled transaction that will remind you to make the card payment before your monthly due date. That will help you avoid those nasty late fees. Set the scheduled transaction up with a variable amount, and tell Quicken to remind you of the transaction, rather than enter it automatically in the register. Then you can edit the transaction to show the amount you will actually pay this month. See Chapter 4 for more information about scheduling transactions.

mortgage setup (Win) p. 96

- You use much the same procedure for setting up other kinds of loans as you do for your mortgage, except that you choose one of the other loan types (Vehicle or Liability) in the first step of the Quicken Account Setup Assistant. You can also set up a loan in the Loans window, which you can reach by choosing Property & Debt > Loans.

extra bits

mortgage setup (Mac) p. 99

- If you checked Schedule payment on Calendar in the Payment Options section of the Set Up Loan dialog, the Financial Calendar opens to allow you to schedule the payment.

make loan payments p. 102

- Loan payments are entered as split transactions. Open the split to see what portion went toward interest and what went to pay down the principal.

track your mortgage p. 104

- You can see the history of a loan by opening the liability account register for the loan.
- You can also get reports of your mortgage activity. See Chapter 8 for more information about reports.

8. create reports and graphs

Quicken's reports and graphs are some of its most powerful tools, because they distill all your numbers and transactions into information that you can use to get a comprehensive picture of your finances. After using Quicken for just a few months, you'll have a good record of how much you are spending and where your money is going. If you have a bit too much credit card debt, you can easily see how much you are spending on credit card interest, which should give you the impetus to pay off those bills.

One of the best features of Quicken reports and graphs is that you can use them to look at your financial data in different ways. You can view your finances in as much or as little detail as you need, and you can pull out just the information that you want. For example, at tax time, I run a report to show all of my tax-deductible expenditures for the previous year, all neatly categorized and totaled. My accountant appreciates it, and because using the reports takes less of his time, it saves me money. The rest of the year, I use reports and graphs to track my income and expenses.

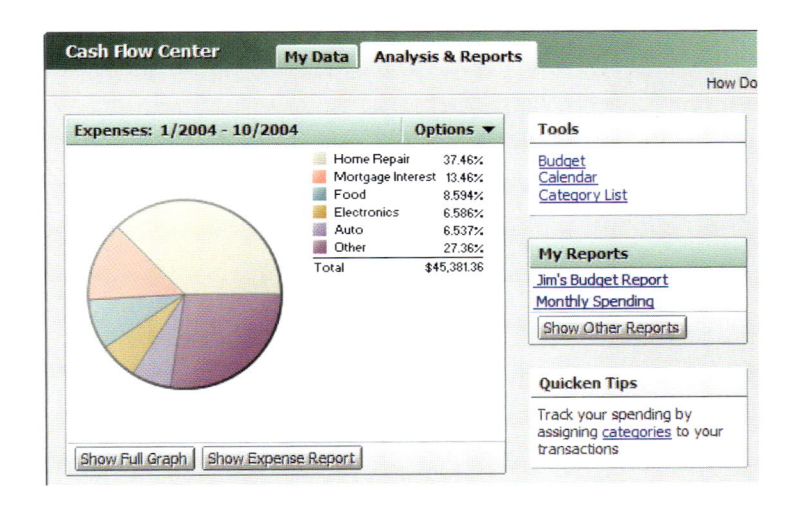

get EasyAnswers

Quicken provides a few different ways to get reports. A good way to find quick answers to your financial questions is through EasyAnswer reports, which answer basic questions such as "Where did I spend my money?" and "What are my investments worth?"

On Windows, choose Reports > EasyAnswer Reports and Graphs. The Reports and Graphs window appears, set to the EasyAnswer tab.

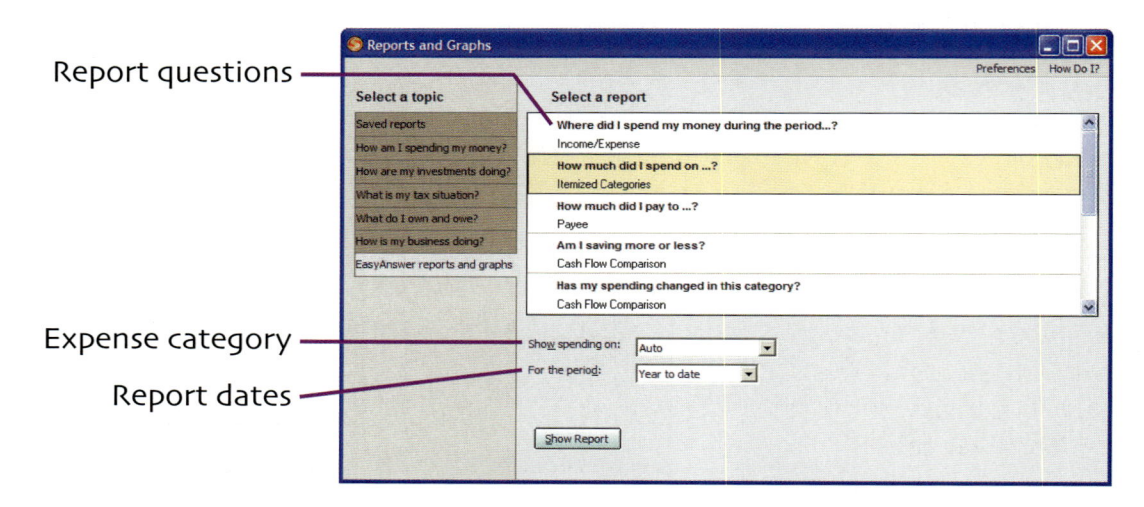

There are ten preconfigured reports in the form of basic questions in the window. Click to select one of them. Depending on which question you choose, the expense category and report dates pop-up menus may change. The report dates menu contains preset time periods for reports.

To get a report, click the report question you want answered, then choose the report date period from the pop-up menu. If the report you chose allows you to select a category, the expense category pop-up menu will appear. Choose the category you want. Click Show Report.

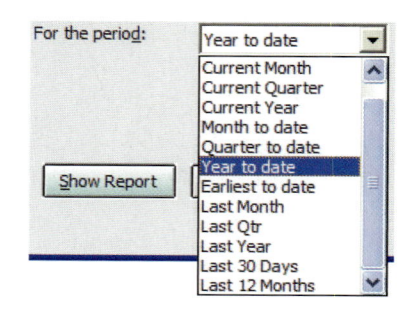

create reports and graphs

You can change the dates the report covers by choosing from the Date Range menu at the top of the report window. The Interval menu shows you subtotals for time periods; for example, you can see your expenses by Year, Month, Quarter, and so forth.

To get an EasyAnswer report on the Mac, click the Reporting tab, then click the Reports button in the toolbar. The Reports window appears. The report appears, set to the EasyAnswer tab.

Click to select the question you want answered, then choose the date range from the pop-up menu. If you picked a question that requires it, choose a category from the pop-up menu next to the question to narrow your report. Click Create. A new window appears with your selected report.

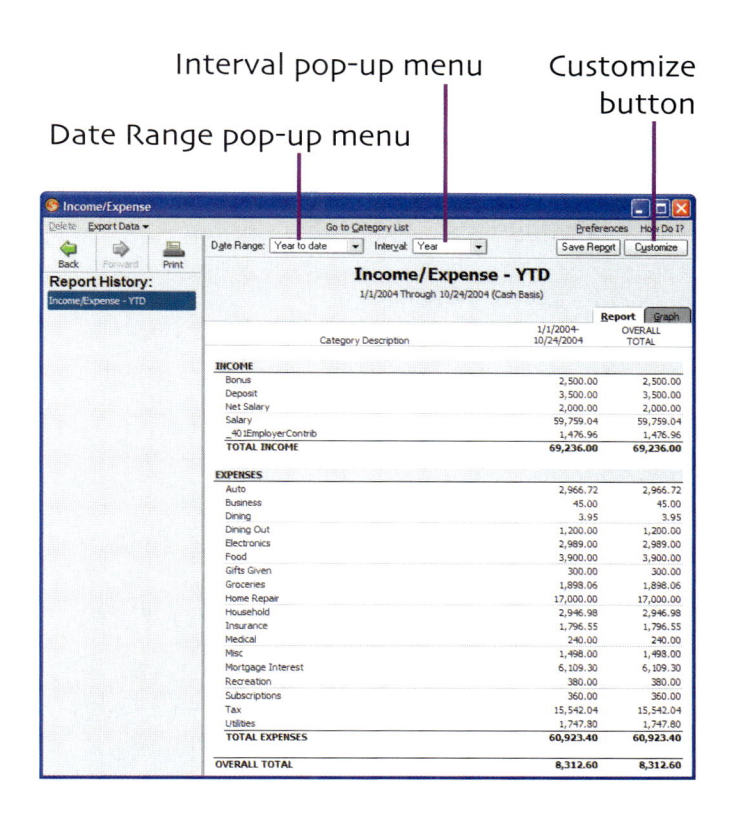

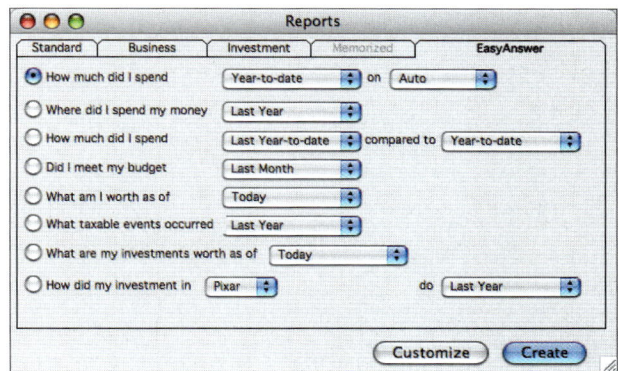

Interval pop-up menu

Date Range pop-up menu

Customize button

create reports and graphs

109

use standard reports

Standard reports give you information such as the details of transactions, net worth, and category transaction reports. Quicken comes with a large number of reports that are ready for you to run.

On Windows, select a standard report by choosing Reports > [report category] > [report name].

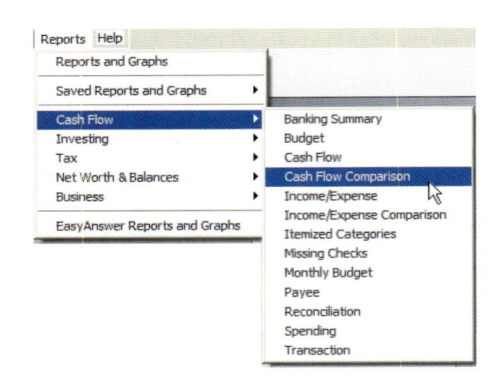

The report opens. You can change the dates the report covers by choosing from the Date Range menu at the top of the report window.

On the Mac, click the Reporting tab, then click the Reports button in the toolbar. The Reports window appears, set to the EasyAnswer tab. Click one of the other tabs (Standard, Business, Investment, or Memorized).

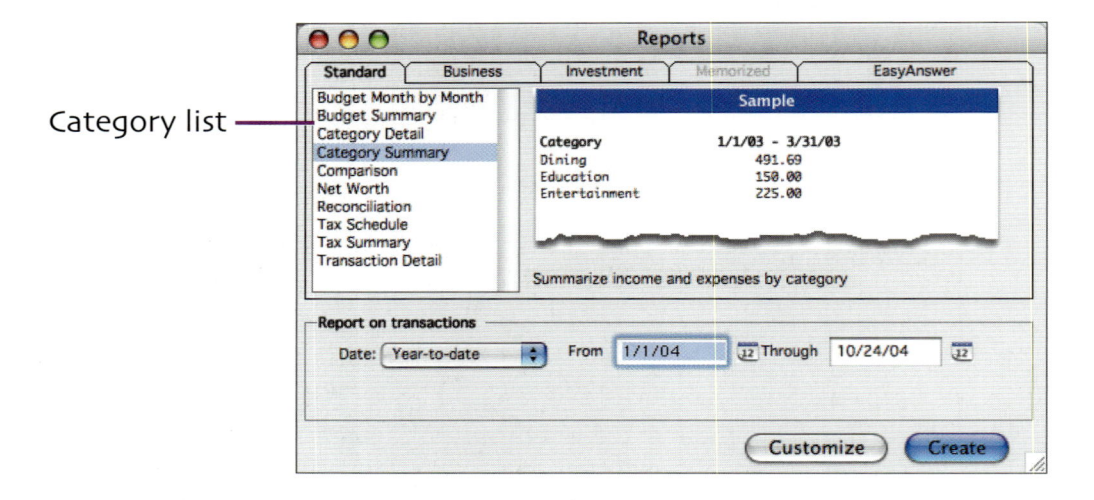

Category list

Click to select the report category from the category list. On the right side of the window, Quicken shows you a sample of the report you selected. Choose from the Date pop-up menu, or enter more specific dates in the From and Through fields. Then click Create. The report opens in a new window.

build custom reports

You can customize a report's details. This is useful when you want to include or exclude certain information. For example, I write books for a living, and I want to know how much money I make per book, and I want to exclude any other income. So I created a custom report that included income just from books. Because I had previously created a separate income category for each book, making the custom report was easy.

To customize a report on Windows, create a standard report of the type you want, then click the Customize button at the top of the report window. The Customize window appears.

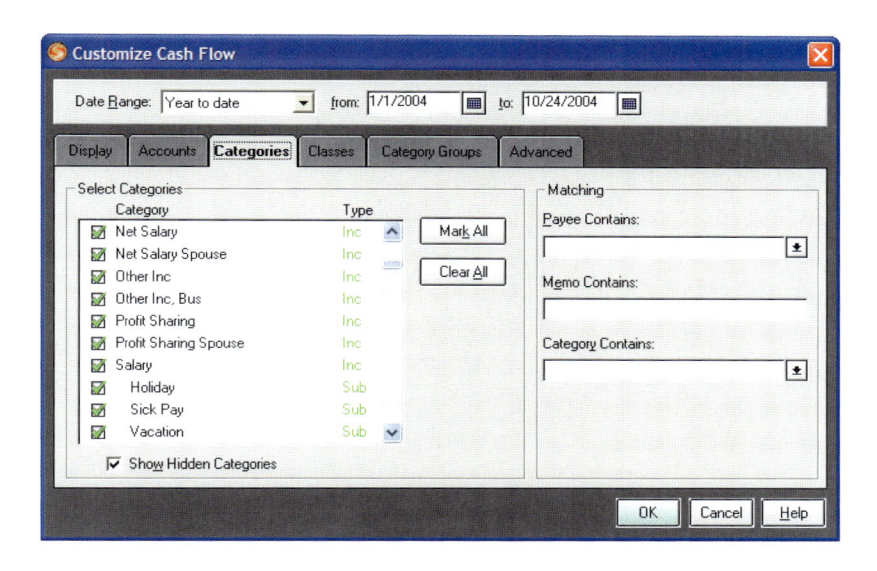

Depending on the kind of report you chose, the Customize window may look different than shown here. Click the different tabs in the Customize window and make choices to customize the report. For example, in the Categories tab of the Customize Cash Flow window shown, I can choose specific categories to include or exclude from the report by selecting or clearing categories in the category list. If I wanted to only include transactions with a particular payee, I would include that payee's name in the Payee Contains field. Experiment until you find the report settings you want, then click OK. The report that was already on your screen will change to match your custom settings.

create reports and graphs 111

build custom reports

To create a custom report on the Mac, open the Reports window, click to select a standard report of the type you want, then click the Customize button at the bottom of the Reports window. The Customize window appears; depending on the kind of report you chose the window may look different than shown here.

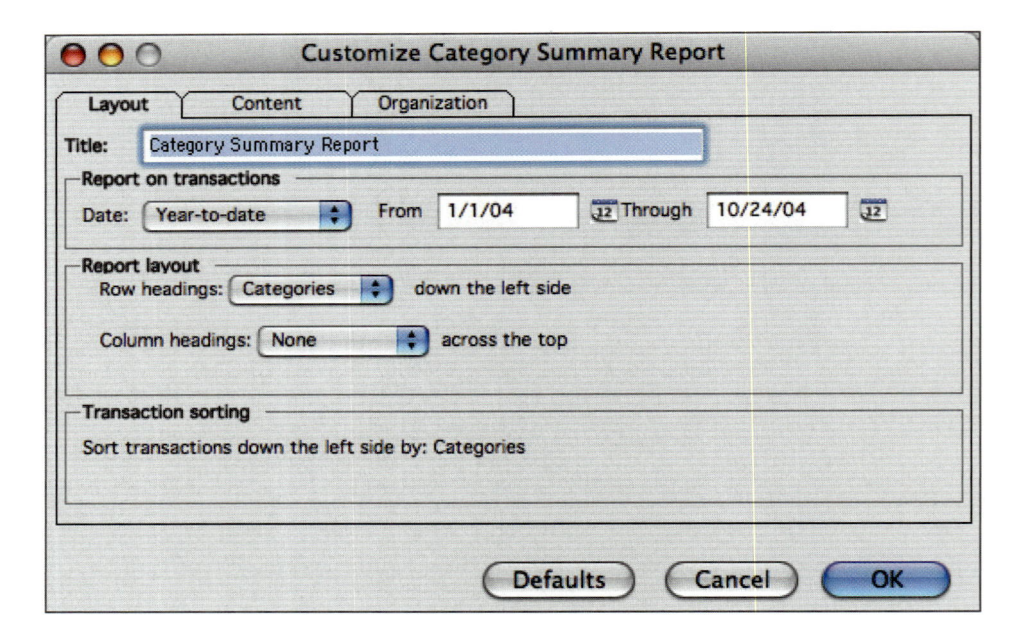

Click the different tabs in the Customize window and make choices to customize the report. Click OK to create the custom report.

save custom reports

Tweaking reports until they're just the way that you want them can take some effort, and it would be a waste of your time if you had to re-create a custom report every time. Instead, you can save custom report settings and reuse them. On Windows, these are called saved reports; on Mac, they are called memorized reports.

Creating saved reports on Windows is easy; when you close a custom report, Quicken automatically asks if you want to save it.

Click Save.

The Save Report dialog appears.

Give the report a name, and choose which of the financial centers you want to save it in. The custom report will appear in the My Reports section of the Analysis & Reports tab of the financial center you select. You can also access them in the Saved Reports and Graphs section of the Reports menu.

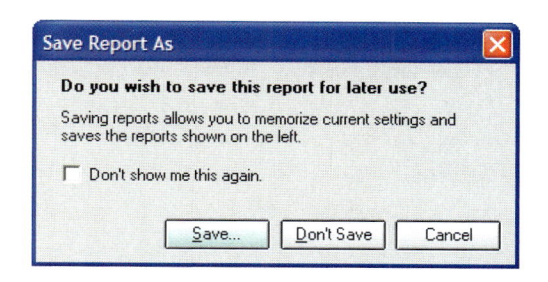

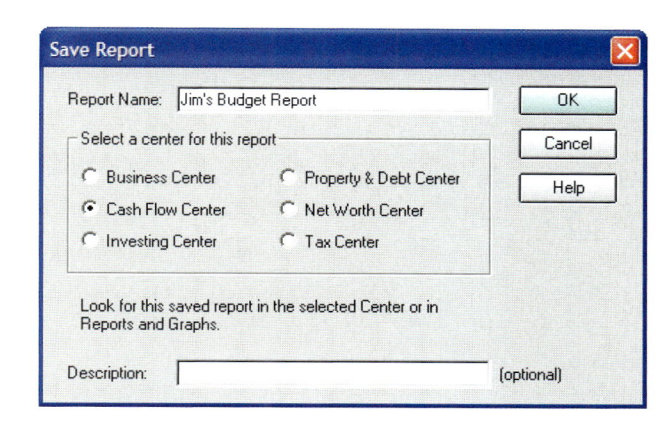

create reports and graphs 113

save custom reports (cont.)

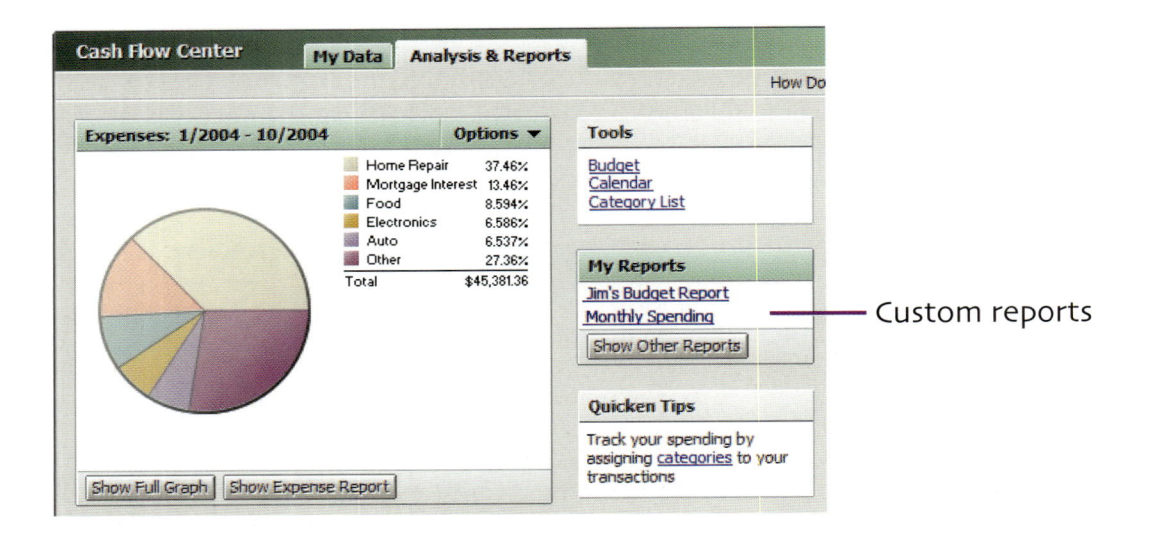

Custom reports

On the Mac, create a custom report, then choose Edit > Memorize. The Memorize Report Template dialog appears.

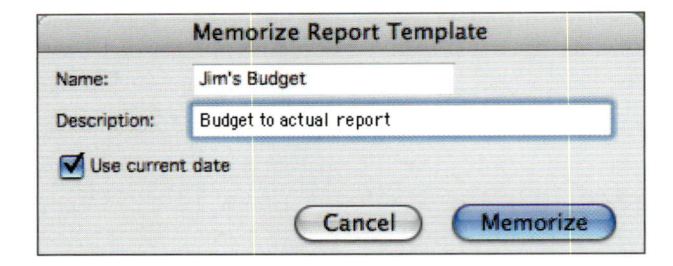

Enter the custom report name, and optionally add a description, then click Memorize. The report will be available for future use in the Memorized tab of the Reports window.

create graphs

When it comes to getting a good overview of your finances, reports are good, but graphs are better. Graphs can often illustrate relationships in your finances that numeric reports don't make clear. Quicken can display your financial data as bar graphs, line graphs, and pie charts to help you quickly analyze your income and expenses, develop budgets, and determine your net worth.

Graphs can also give you an important emotional boost, as I discovered while working to pay off my own consumer debt. I created a bar graph that showed how much debt I owed. Every month, as I made payments, I checked the graph to see how much the debt bar had shrunk. It felt great to see the downward trend as I worked towards my goal, and it felt even better the month that the bar finally hit the zero mark.

To get graphs on Windows, choose Reports > Reports and Graphs. The Reports and Graphs window appears. Click to choose the category that you want from the Select a topic list on the left side of the window, then click to select the particular report you want from the Select a report list. Not all reports have associated graphs; the ones that do have a Show Graph button at the bottom of the window.

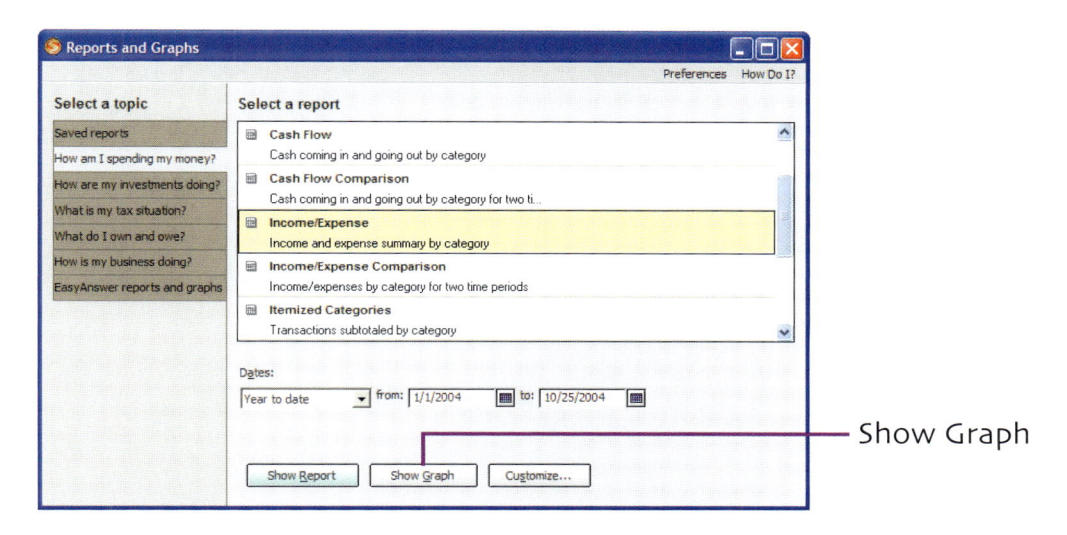

— Show Graph

create reports and graphs

create graphs (cont.)

Choose the date range for the graph in the Dates section of the window, then click Show Graph. The graph appears in a new window.

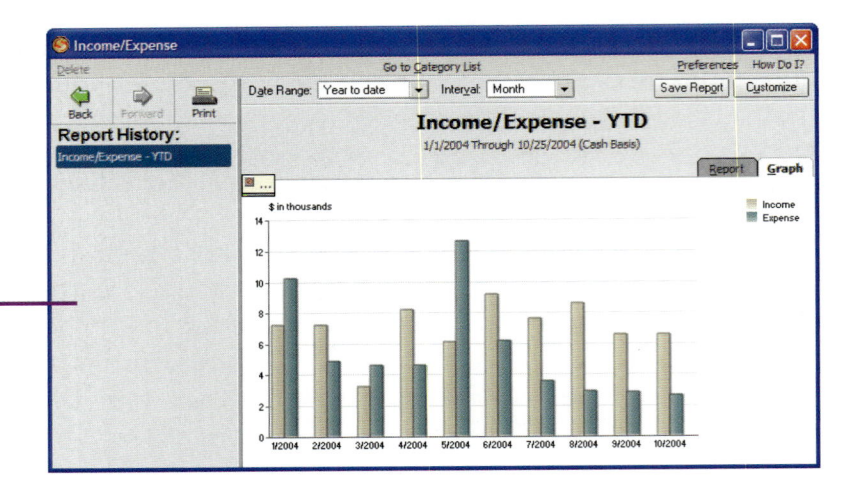

On the Mac, click the Reporting tab, then click the Graphs button in the toolbar. The Graphs window appears.

Click the tab (Standard, Memorized, or EasyAnswer) for the kind of graph you want, then click to select the graph. Click Create to open the window with a new graph.

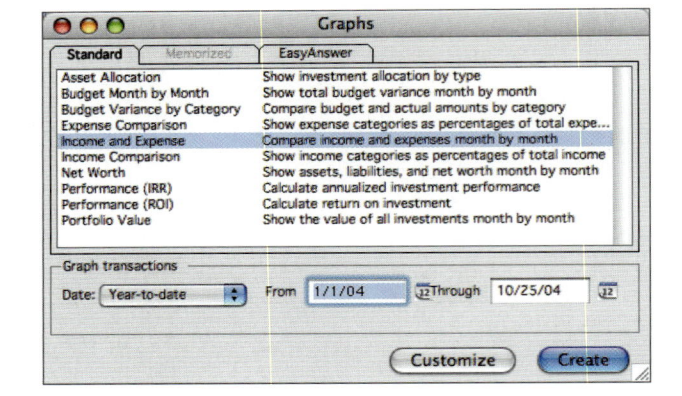

116   **create reports and graphs**

print reports or graphs

Sometimes you'll want to print the report or graph. In either case, begin by creating the report or graph that you want.

On Windows, click the Print button at the top of the report or graph window.

The Print dialog appears. Make any adjustments to the print job you desire, then click OK.

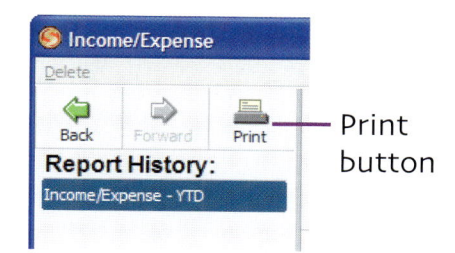

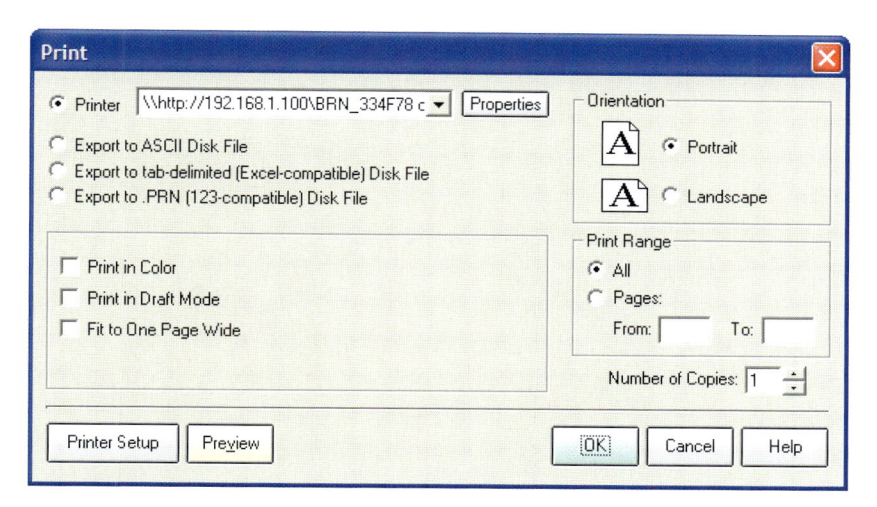

— Print button

On the Mac, with the report or graph window open, choose File > Print Report or File > Print Graph (the menu item changes to match the kind of window you have open). The Print dialog appears. Click Print.

create reports and graphs 117

extra bits

use standard reports p. 110

- When creating reports, one of the options you have for setting the time period of a report is "year-to-date." This just means that it covers the time period from January 1 to today's date. Some reports also offer the option of "last year-to-date," which gives you a report including information from January 1 of last year to the corresponding date from last year that is the same as today's date. This is a great way to find out if your finances are better or worse off than they were at the same time one year ago.

- On almost all reports or graphs, you can use Quicken's Quick-Zoom feature to examine the information in your reports or graphs in greater detail. If you're viewing a report that summarizes the amounts from a category, you can double-click an amount and QuickZoom will take you to another report that shows more detail about the item you selected.

To use QuickZoom, create a report or graph, then move the cursor over one of the amounts in the report (or one of the graph segments) until the cursor turns into a magnifying glass.

EXPENSES	
Uncategorized	0.00
Auto	🔍 577.83
Business	0.00

Double-click the report amount or the graph segment. A new report or graph opens showing you details of the item you clicked.

save custom reports p. 113

- When you attempt to close a report that you have customized, Quicken will ask if you want to save the report. If you do many custom reports that you don't want to save, you can turn the message off by clicking the Don't show me this again button in the alert dialog.

9. set up and track investments

For the vast majority of us, the key to comfortable living in future years and a stress-free retirement is a solid and consistent savings and investment program. Quicken lets you update current market values and see whether you are earning or losing money on your investments.

Investments in Quicken are contained in a *portfolio*, which in turn can contain one or more *securities*. A security can be a single mutual fund, stocks, bonds, or a collection of investments that you have in a brokerage account.

In this chapter, you'll learn how to set up and add to an investment portfolio in Quicken, such as the kind of portfolio you would manage in an IRA or 401(k) account.

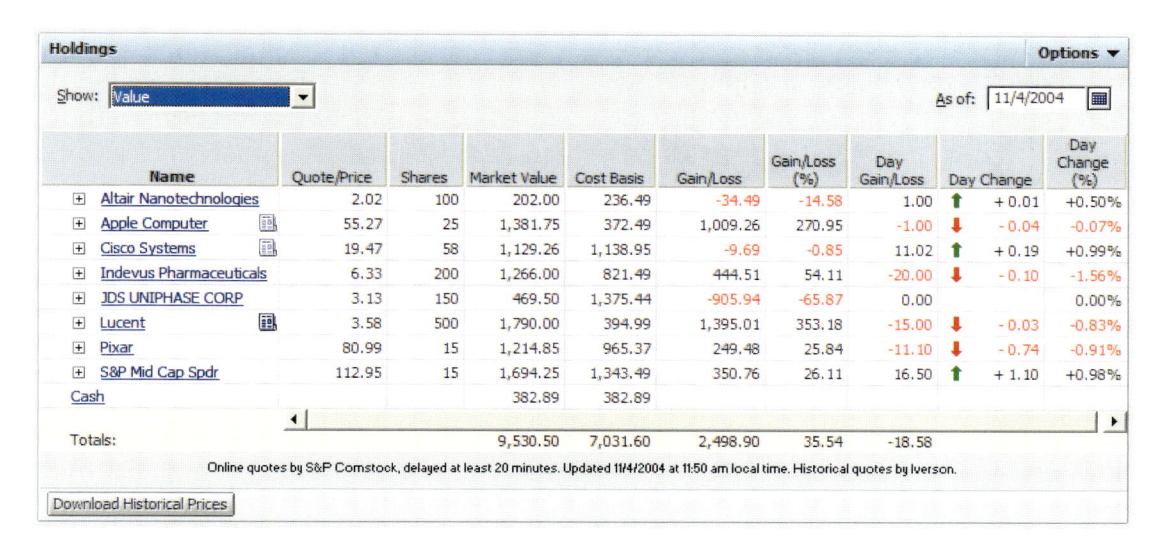

Name	Quote/Price	Shares	Market Value	Cost Basis	Gain/Loss	Gain/Loss (%)	Day Gain/Loss	Day Change	Day Change (%)
Altair Nanotechnologies	2.02	100	202.00	236.49	-34.49	-14.58	1.00	+0.01	+0.50%
Apple Computer	55.27	25	1,381.75	372.49	1,009.26	270.95	-1.00	-0.04	-0.07%
Cisco Systems	19.47	58	1,129.26	1,138.95	-9.69	-0.85	11.02	+0.19	+0.99%
Indevus Pharmaceuticals	6.33	200	1,266.00	821.49	444.51	54.11	-20.00	-0.10	-1.56%
JDS UNIPHASE CORP	3.13	150	469.50	1,375.44	-905.94	-65.87	0.00		0.00%
Lucent	3.58	500	1,790.00	394.99	1,395.01	353.18	-15.00	-0.03	-0.83%
Pixar	80.99	15	1,214.85	965.37	249.48	25.84	-11.10	-0.74	-0.91%
S&P Mid Cap Spdr	112.95	15	1,694.25	1,343.49	350.76	26.11	16.50	+1.10	+0.98%
Cash			382.89	382.89					
Totals:			9,530.50	7,031.60	2,498.90	35.54	-18.58		

119

how much detail?

Before you get started setting up your portfolio account, you need to decide how much investment history to include in your records. You have three options: enter a complete history, just this year's information, or your current investment holdings.

Of the three options, the complete history requires the most data entry, because you'll need to enter the initial purchase price for each security and all of the subsequent transactions. The benefit of this approach is that all of your reports are complete and Quicken can accurately calculate capital gains and losses. Because a large portion of the benefit of tracking your investments in Quicken is knowing how much money you have made or lost, this is the approach that I recommend.

If you have a financial institution that allows you to download information over the Internet directly into Quicken, much of your data entry will be eliminated. I highly recommend this. You'll know that your financial institution can download into Quicken because the name of the financial institution will appear during Quicken Account Setup.

Here are the pros and cons of the two methods of portfolio setup that I do not recommend. If you decide to enter just the current year's data, you'll enter the investment balances as of the end of last year and then enter all of the transactions for each security since the beginning of this year. The good thing about this method is that the information you need to find and enter is more recent and probably easier for you to obtain. Reports that deal with events from this year will be accurate, and if you sell a security, Quicken will be able to track which lots of the security you should sell to minimize or maximize your short-term capital gains. The downside of this method is that Quicken will not know the original cost of the security (called the cost basis), so you can't get accurate long-term capital gains or realized gain reports.

If you decide to enter just your current investment holdings, it will take the least amount of time, because all you have to do is enter information from your latest investment statement. The significant drawback is that data for this year and past years will be incomplete, and you won't be able to get reports for capital gains or realized gains.

set up and track investments

portfolio setup (Win)

To create a portfolio account on Windows, begin by choosing Investing > Investing Accounts > Add Account. The Quicken Account Setup window appears, asking you to specify the financial institution for the account.

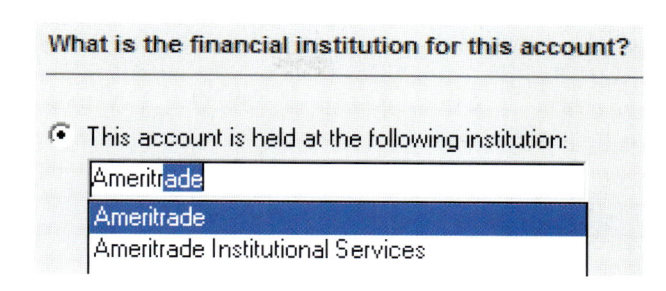

Type in the name of the financial institution. Quicken will try to find the institution in its internal financial institutions list and will enter matches as you type. Click Next when your financial institution appears. If Quicken is unfamiliar with your financial institution, you'll see one more screen that asks you to confirm the name you entered.

Next, you'll be asked if you want to set up your account online or manually. Make your choice, then click Next.

If you clicked Online and your financial institution is one of Quicken's download partners, the next screen you see will ask you to enter your account number and PIN that was provided to you by your financial institution.

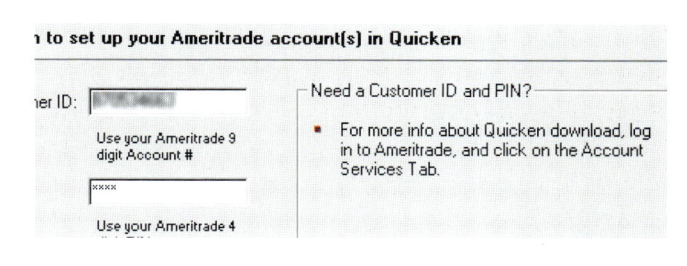

Enter the information, and click Next. Quicken connects to the Internet and downloads setup information about the account, then asks you to give the account a name. Do so, then click Next.

You'll see a summary screen with the information you entered. Click Done. Quicken will connect to your financial institution again to download transactions (most financial institutions keep the past 60–180 days online) and will confirm the account's proper setup in the Online Summary window. Click Done.

set up and track investments

portfolio setup (Win)

The account will open, displaying the account holdings. Quicken makes placeholder entries for the current values of the securities in your account. Quicken does not download the cost basis for the holdings, so you should enter the transactions from your account statements that correspond to the placeholder entries, then delete the placeholders.

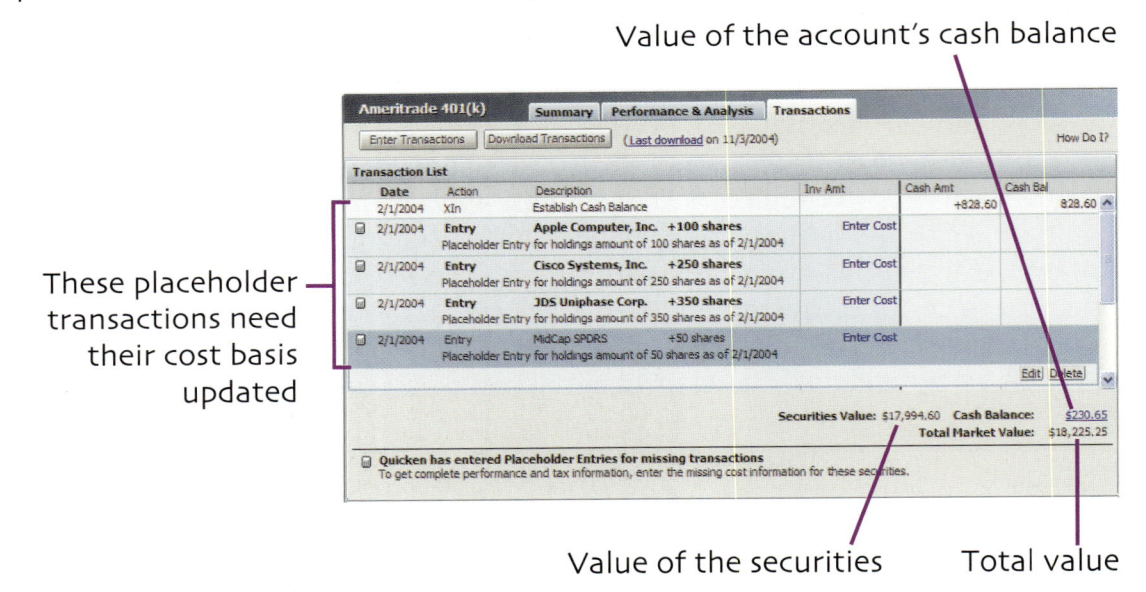

Value of the account's cash balance

These placeholder transactions need their cost basis updated

Value of the securities   Total value

If you chose to set up the account manually, Quicken will ask you to specify the type of investment account (Standard Brokerage, IRA or Keogh, 401(k) or 403(b), or Single Mutual Fund). Choose the type you want, then click Next.

The next screen differs, depending on the type of investment account you chose, but it will ask you to provide a name and information related to the account. Enter the information, then click Next.

On the next screen, enter information about the cash balance in the account, taken from your latest statement or from the financial institution's Web site. Click Next.

set up and track investments

Next, you should enter the ticker symbols of the securities in the account. Quicken will use these symbols to download security details and prices later. If you don't know the ticker symbols, click the Ticker Symbol Lookup button, and your Web browser will open and allow you to find the symbol. Enter each ticker symbol and the name of the security, then click Next.

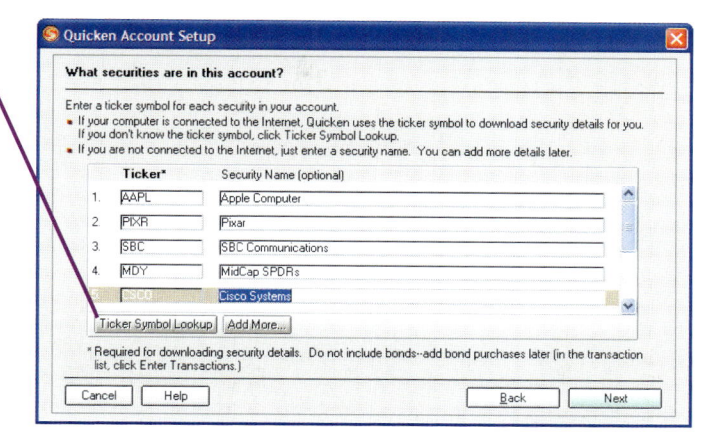

Quicken will connect to the Internet, confirm the symbols, and will then ask you to enter your current holdings for each security. Enter the number of shares you own for each security, and click the button to indicate if the security is a stock, mutual fund, or other security type. When you are done, click Next.

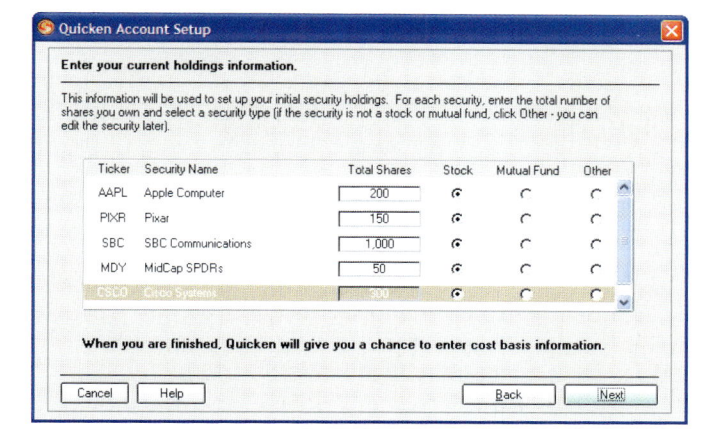

set up and track investments

portfolio setup (Win)

A summary screen appears, allowing you to check your work. If it is correct, click Done. If you made a mistake, click Back and fix the error. When you are done, the account's holdings screen appears, with the current information about the account. Once again, you should enter the cost basis for each security by clicking the Enter links in the Cost Basis column.

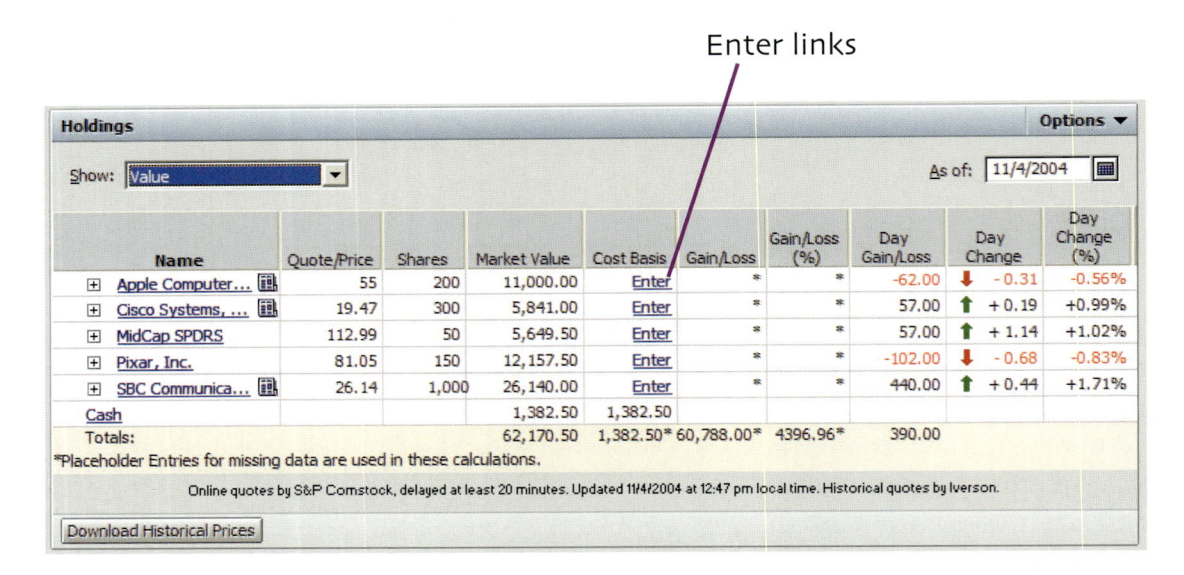

Enter links

Name	Quote/Price	Shares	Market Value	Cost Basis	Gain/Loss	Gain/Loss (%)	Day Gain/Loss	Day Change	Day Change (%)
Apple Computer...	55	200	11,000.00	Enter	*	*	-62.00	-0.31	-0.56%
Cisco Systems, ...	19.47	300	5,841.00	Enter	*	*	57.00	+0.19	+0.99%
MidCap SPDRS	112.99	50	5,649.50	Enter	*	*	57.00	+1.14	+1.02%
Pixar, Inc.	81.05	150	12,157.50	Enter	*	*	-102.00	-0.68	-0.83%
SBC Communica...	26.14	1,000	26,140.00	Enter	*	*	440.00	+0.44	+1.71%
Cash			1,382.50	1,382.50					
Totals:			62,170.50	1,382.50*	60,788.00*	4396.96*	390.00		

*Placeholder Entries for missing data are used in these calculations.

Online quotes by S&P Comstock, delayed at least 20 minutes. Updated 11/4/2004 at 12:47 pm local time. Historical quotes by Iverson.

Show: Value   As of: 11/4/2004

[Download Historical Prices]

set up and track investments

portfolio setup (Mac)

To create a portfolio account on the Mac, click the Investing tab in the toolbar, then choose File > New Account. The New Account Assistant window appears, asking you to specify the financial institution for the account.

There are only a limited number of financial institutions supported on the Mac for online brokerage access; see page 132 for a list. If your institution is on the list, select it and click Continue. If your financial institution does not appear on the list, select This account is not held at one of the financial institutions listed above, and then click Continue.

On the next screen, in the Investments section, choose the kind of investment account you want to set up, then click Continue.

You're next asked to give the account a name. Type it into the Account name field, then click Continue.

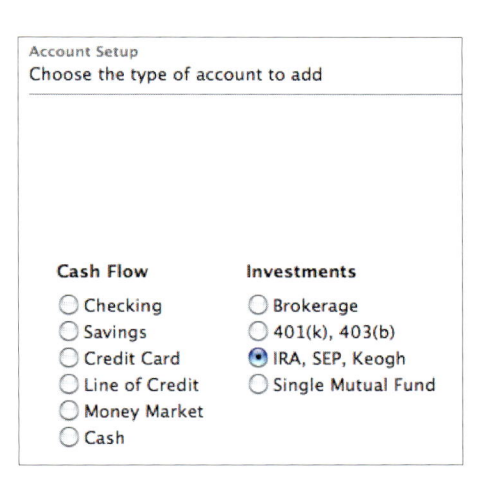

set up and track investments

125

portfolio setup (Mac)

Enter the last statement date, then if the account has a cash balance, enter it in the Cash balance field. Click Continue.

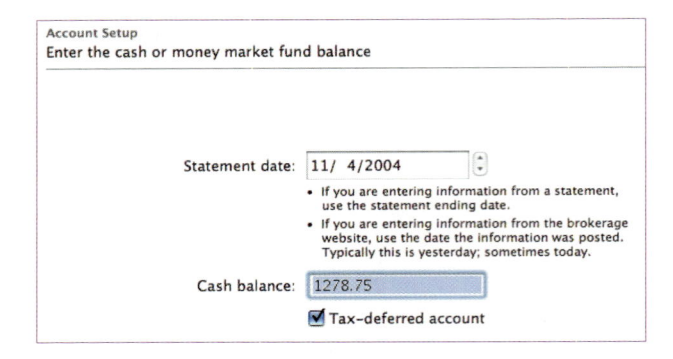

On the next screen, you'll enter your current holdings in this account. Click the Add button. A dialog will slide down from the top of the window. Enter the security name, its ticker symbol, the number of shares held, the purchase date, and the price per share when you bought it. Only the security name and the number of shares held are required at this time; you can go back and add the additional details later. Click OK. The information you added appears in the window. If you have more holdings to add, click the Add button again. Otherwise, click Continue.

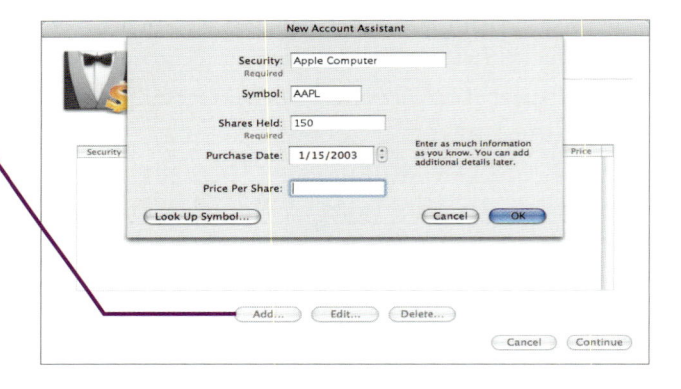

The register for the new Portfolio account opens.

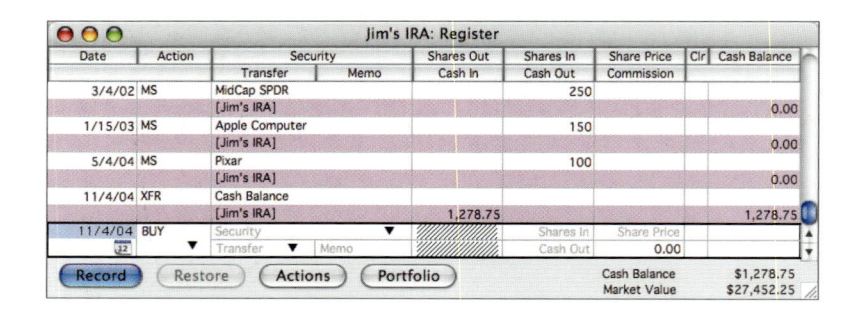

126

set up and track investments

use portfolio window

The Portfolio window is your main management tool for your investments. You can use it to see the overall value of your investments at a glance; sort your investments in different ways; see how much your investments are worth today, or at anytime in the past; and even track the prices of securities that you don't yet own, but wish to keep an eye on. The Portfolio window is an important tool for analyzing how well your investment strategy is working.

To view your Portfolio on Windows, click to select the investment account in the Account Bar, then click the Summary tab. In the default Value view, you'll see a list of the securities held in the account, along with the current price, the amount of shares owned, gains and losses, and so forth.

Show menu

Name	Quote/Price	Shares	Market Value	Cost Basis	Gain/Loss	Gain/Loss (%)	Day Gain/Loss	Day Change	Day Change (%)
Altair Nanotechnologies	2.02	100	202.00	236.49	-34.49	-14.58	1.00 ↑	+0.01	+0.50%
Apple Computer	55.27	25	1,381.75	372.49	1,009.26	270.95	-1.00 ↓	-0.04	-0.07%
Cisco Systems	19.47	58	1,129.26	1,138.95	-9.69	-0.85	11.02 ↑	+0.19	+0.99%
Indevus Pharmaceuticals	6.33	200	1,266.00	821.49	444.51	54.11	-20.00 ↓	-0.10	-1.56%
JDS UNIPHASE CORP	3.13	150	469.50	1,375.44	-905.94	-65.87	0.00		0.00%
Lucent	3.58	500	1,790.00	394.99	1,395.01	353.18	-15.00 ↓	-0.03	-0.83%
Pixar	80.99	15	1,214.85	965.37	249.48	25.84	-11.10 ↓	-0.74	-0.91%
S&P Mid Cap Spdr	112.95	15	1,694.25	1,343.49	350.76	26.11	16.50 ↑	+1.10	+0.98%
Cash			382.89	382.89					
Totals:			9,530.50	7,031.60	2,498.90	35.54	-18.58		

To see the performance of your portfolio, choose either Recent performance or Historic performance from the Show menu. The view changes to show you how well the investments have been doing.

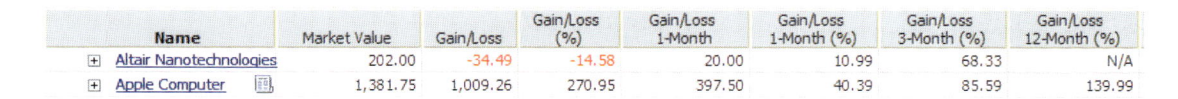

Name	Market Value	Gain/Loss	Gain/Loss (%)	Gain/Loss 1-Month	Gain/Loss 1-Month (%)	Gain/Loss 3-Month (%)	Gain/Loss 12-Month (%)
Altair Nanotechnologies	202.00	-34.49	-14.58	20.00	10.99	68.33	N/A
Apple Computer	1,381.75	1,009.26	270.95	397.50	40.39	85.59	139.99

set up and track investments

use portfolio window

You can also see a graph of your investment performance; click the Performance & Analysis tab of the Portfolio account.

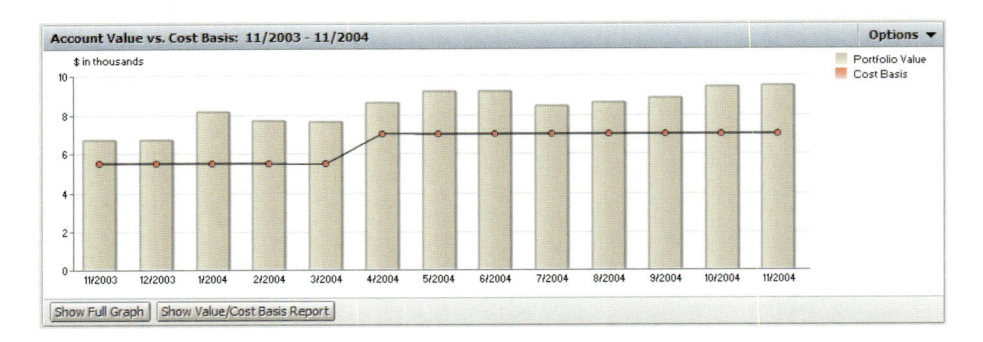

On the Mac, click the Investing tab on the toolbar, then click the Portfolio button. The Portfolio window appears.

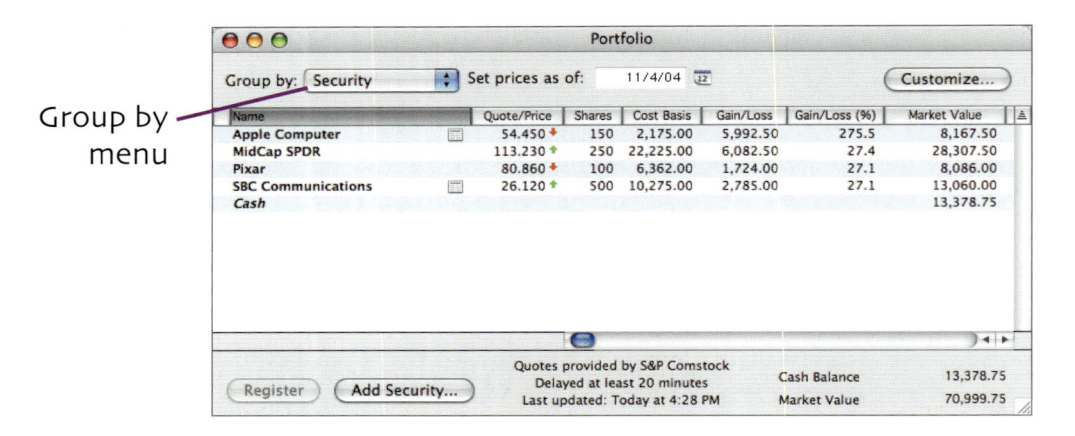

Group by menu

To change the Portfolio view, you can change the Group by pop-up menu. You can sort the contents of the window by Account (which lets you see the securities contained in multiple investment accounts); Security (which consolidates all of your securities in an alphabetical list view); Type (which shows the securities sorted by type, such as Bond, Mutual Fund, and Stock); or Asset Class (this sorts the securities by how large the companies or funds are).

set up and track investments

view security details

Another way to work with the securities in your Portfolio window is to zoom in on individual securities to get more information. The security details include the setup information for the security; a graph of the security's performance; and a list of the transactions that you have made with that security.

To view security details on Windows, click the portfolio account in the Account Bar, then click the Summary tab. In the list of securities, the date of the security will be blue and underlined, indicating that it is a link. Click the link. The security detail window opens.

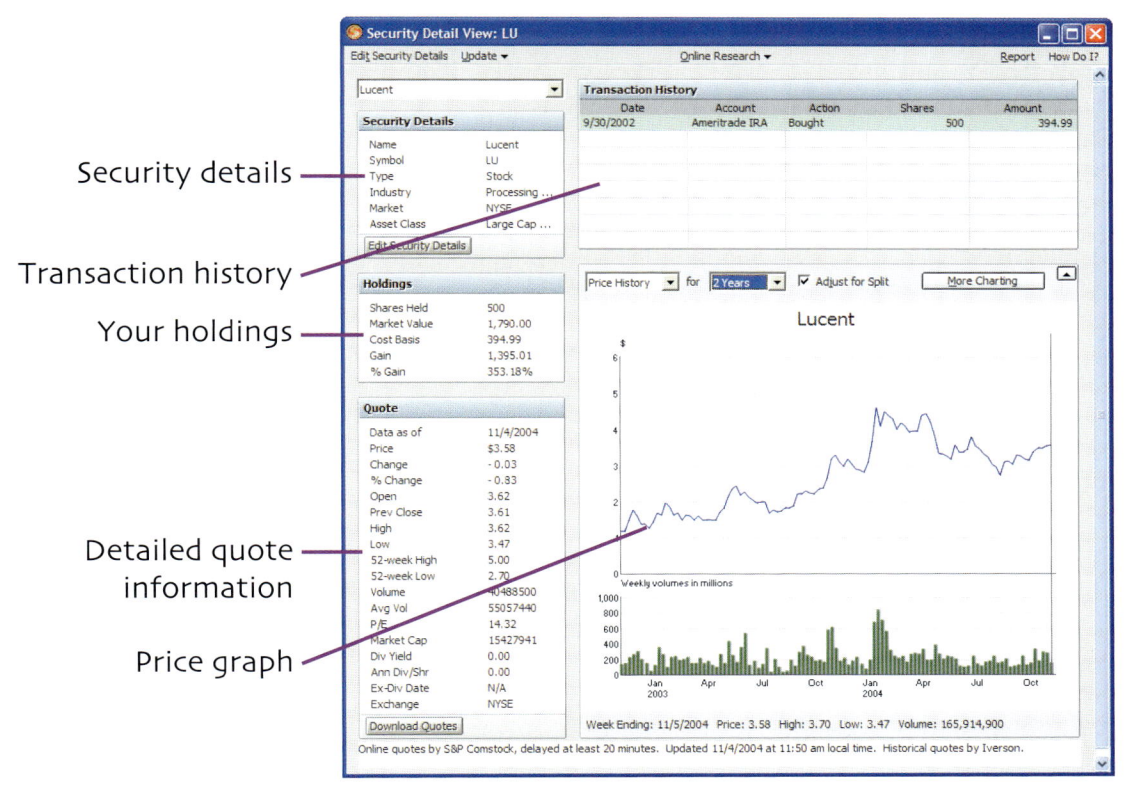

- Security details
- Transaction history
- Your holdings
- Detailed quote information
- Price graph

Security details in Windows

set up and track investments 129

view security details

On the Mac, click the Investing tab on the toolbar, then click the Portfolio button on the toolbar. In the Portfolio window, double-click the name of the security for which you want detail. The Security Detail window appears. Click the different tabs in the Security Detail window to see the Setup Info, Graph, Prices, or Transactions.

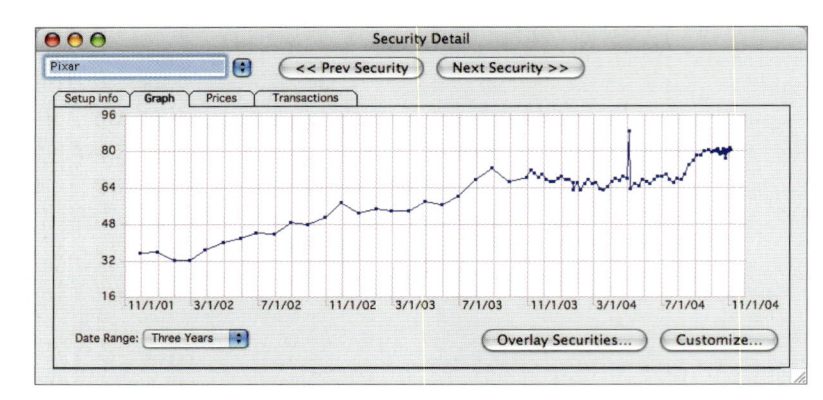

Security details in Macintosh

130 set up and track investments

download quotes

In order for your investment information to be up-to-date, you'll need to periodically download current security prices to your portfolio. Normally, downloading security prices will be just one of the tasks included when you do a One Step Update (see Chapter 5 for more on One Step Update), but it is also possible to get security price quotes without doing your other on-line activities.

To download security price quotes on Windows, choose Investing > Online Activities > Download Quotes. The One Step Update window appears, showing you the download progress. Your Portfolio will update to display the latest price quotes.

On the Mac, choose Online > Update Security Prices. The Quicken Quotes Progress window appears reporting the download progress.

The Portfolio window will update to display the latest price quotes.

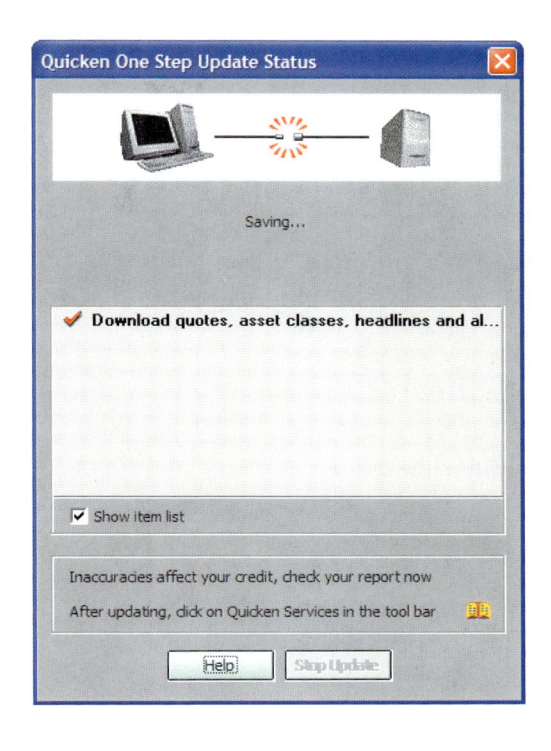

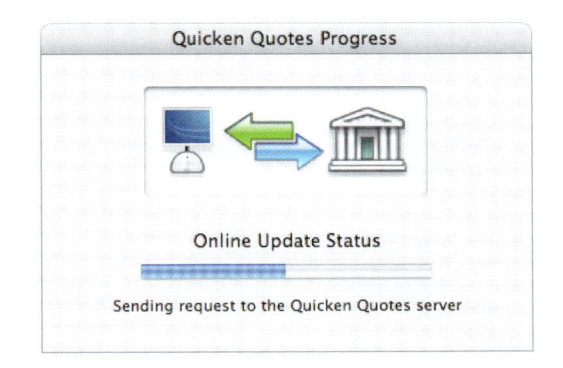

set up and track investments

extra bits

portfolio setup (Win) p. 121

- To see a list of all of the financial institutions that Quicken for Windows supports, choose Online > Participating Financial Institutions. A browser window opens with the list.

portfolio setup (Mac) p. 125

- To see a list of all of the financial institutions that Quicken for Macintosh supports, choose Online > Financial Institutions. The Financial Institutions window appears. To update the list with the latest information (new financial institutions are being added all the time), click the Update List button at the bottom of the window.

- Unfortunately, there are far fewer financial institutions that can download brokerage transactions directly into Quicken for Mac than can do so with Quicken for Windows. At press time, that list included 11 institutions: A.G. Edwards, Charles Schwab & Company, CSFB Private Client Services, Fidelity Investments, Harrisdirect, Morgan Keegan & Company, Northern Trust, RBC Dain Rauscher, TD Waterhouse, TIAA-CREF, and Wells Fargo Investments.

download quotes p. 131

- You can download prices as many times a day as you wish, but Quicken stores only one price per day, the last price you downloaded.

- Prices for stocks, options, and indexes are updated constantly during the business day, although the quotes you get online are delayed from real-time by about 20 minutes. Prices for mutual funds are updated only once per day at 6 p.m. Eastern time.

10. manage investments

After setting up your investment portfolio (see Chapter 9), you'll need to manage your investments on an ongoing basis. That means updating the share prices of your securities and making entries whenever you buy or sell an investment. You learned how to download security prices at the end of the last chapter, and this chapter will show you how to enter investment transactions in Quicken when you buy and sell securities. You'll also learn how to deal with transactions that aren't tied to a purchase or sale, such as when a security pays a dividend.

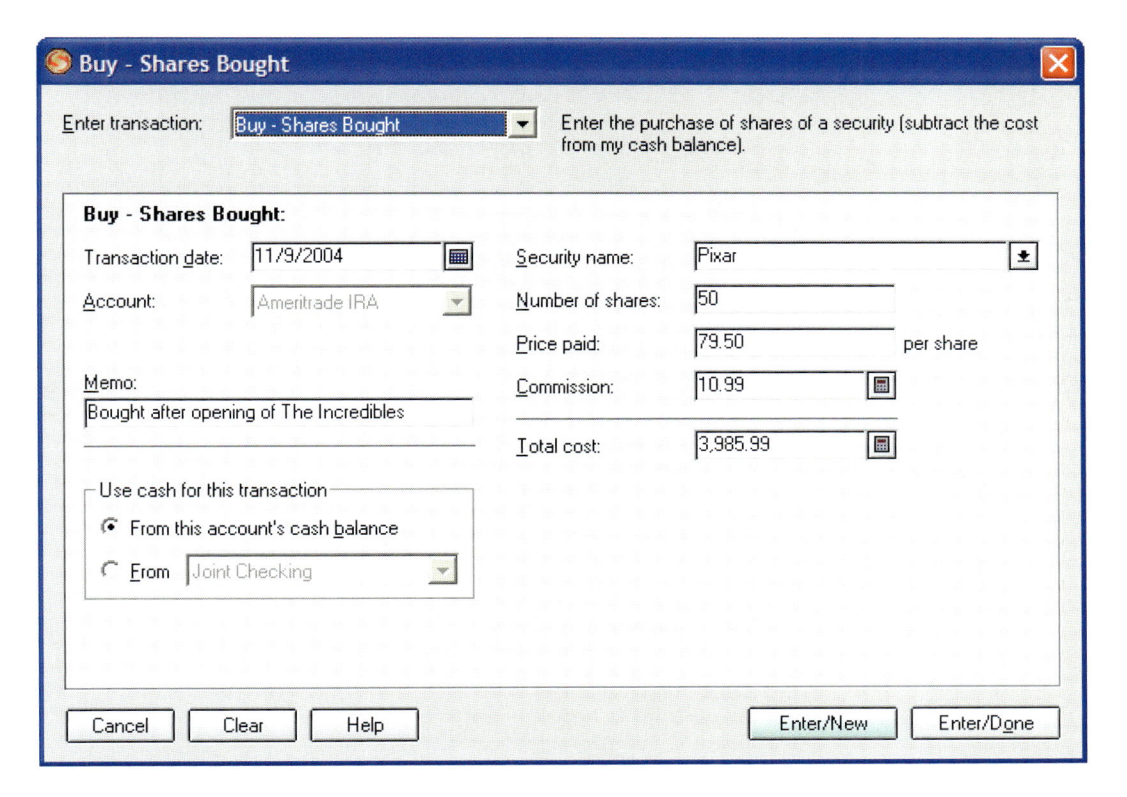

add transactions (Win)

Because entering security transactions can be a bit involved, Quicken uses special dialogs to walk you through the process. These dialogs ensure that you will enter all of the information that Quicken needs to properly track the transaction.

On Windows, begin by clicking to select the investment account in the Account Bar. Towards the top of the window, click Enter Transactions.

The Investment Transactions dialog appears. The contents of this dialog will change, depending on the investment action selected from the Enter transaction pop-up menu, and whether the account is a single mutual fund or a portfolio account. This example is for purchasing shares of a stock in a portfolio account. Of course, if you want another kind of transaction, you should choose it from the Enter transaction pop-up menu.

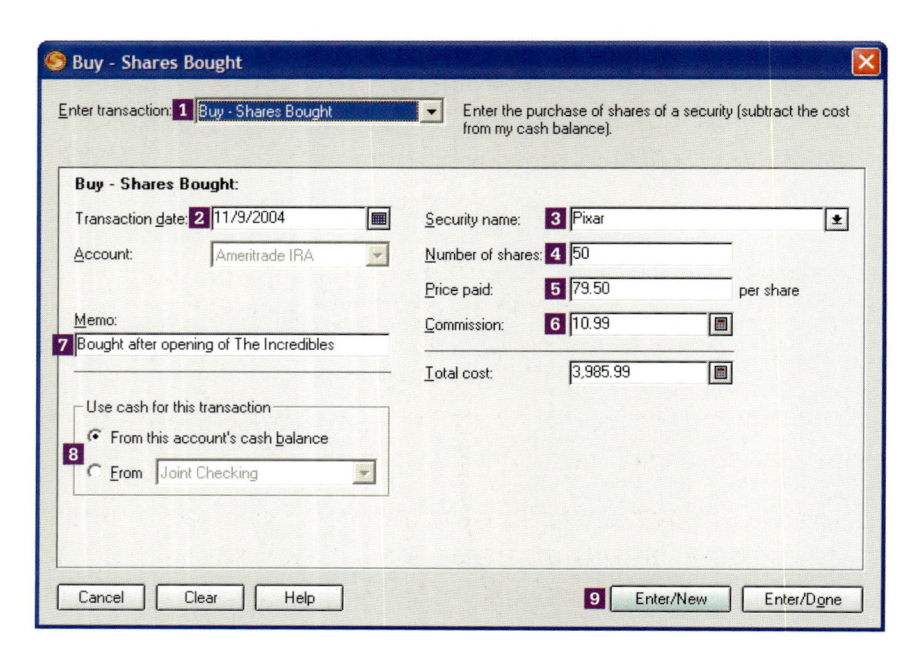

134 manage investments

1 Choose Buy – Shares Bought from the investment transactions pop-up menu.

2 Enter the Transaction date.

3 Choose the security you want to purchase from the Security name pop-up menu. This menu lists all the securities you have previously bought. If you are buying a security that is new to your portfolio, click the Add New Security button at the bottom of the pop-up menu, and Quicken will walk you through a quick Wizard to add the new security.

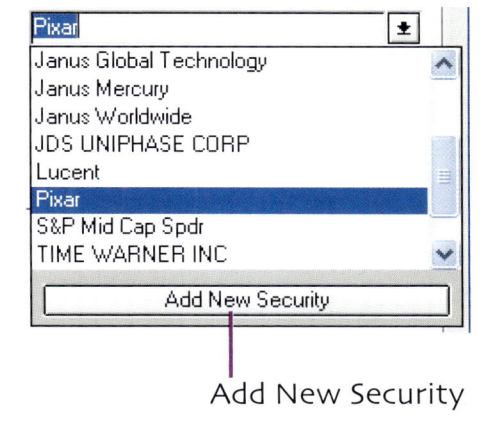

Add New Security

4 Enter the number of shares you have bought in the Number of shares field.

5 Enter the price you paid per share in the Price paid field.

6 If you paid a broker commission, enter its dollar amount in the Commission field. Quicken calculates the cost of the transaction (number of shares times price per share plus commission) and places the result in the Total cost field.

7 If you want to add a memo, type it in the Memo field.

8 The money to pay for your purchase can either come from the cash balance in your portfolio account or from another Quicken account, such as your checking account. If it comes from the portfolio cash balance, in the Use cash for this transaction section, click From this account's cash balance. If the money comes from another account, click From, and then choose the account from the pop-up menu next to it.

9 If you want to save the current transaction and immediately enter another, click Enter/New. If you are done entering transactions, click Enter/Done. The investment transaction is saved, and it appears in the Transactions tab of the investment account.

manage investments

add transactions (Mac)

On the Mac, you enter investment transactions using the Investment Actions window. This lists all of the possible investment transactions.

Begin by clicking the Investing tab on the toolbar, then clicking the Portfolio button, which opens the Portfolio window. If you instead want to do an investment action on a single mutual fund account, choose the account from the Registers pop-up menu on the toolbar, and its register will open.

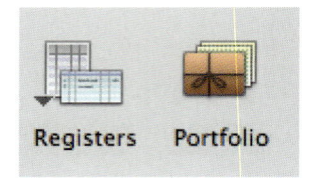

Choose Activities > Investment Actions. The Investment Actions window appears. Double-click the investment action you want, and the associated action form appears.

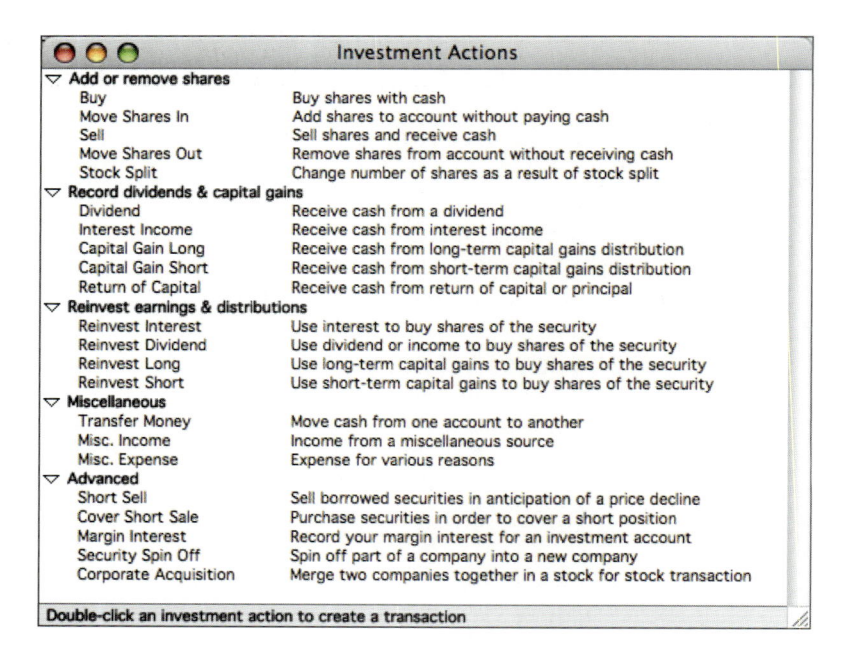

Investment Actions	
▽ **Add or remove shares**	
Buy	Buy shares with cash
Move Shares In	Add shares to account without paying cash
Sell	Sell shares and receive cash
Move Shares Out	Remove shares from account without receiving cash
Stock Split	Change number of shares as a result of stock split
▽ **Record dividends & capital gains**	
Dividend	Receive cash from a dividend
Interest Income	Receive cash from interest income
Capital Gain Long	Receive cash from long-term capital gains distribution
Capital Gain Short	Receive cash from short-term capital gains distribution
Return of Capital	Receive cash from return of capital or principal
▽ **Reinvest earnings & distributions**	
Reinvest Interest	Use interest to buy shares of the security
Reinvest Dividend	Use dividend or income to buy shares of the security
Reinvest Long	Use long-term capital gains to buy shares of the security
Reinvest Short	Use short-term capital gains to buy shares of the security
▽ **Miscellaneous**	
Transfer Money	Move cash from one account to another
Misc. Income	Income from a miscellaneous source
Misc. Expense	Expense for various reasons
▽ **Advanced**	
Short Sell	Sell borrowed securities in anticipation of a price decline
Cover Short Sale	Purchase securities in order to cover a short position
Margin Interest	Record your margin interest for an investment account
Security Spin Off	Spin off part of a company into a new company
Corporate Acquisition	Merge two companies together in a stock for stock transaction

Double-click an investment action to create a transaction

1 Choose the investment account from the Account pop-up menu.

2 Enter the transaction date.

3 Enter the number of shares you bought.

4 Choose the security you want to purchase from the pop-up menu next to *Of*. This menu lists all the securities you have previously bought. If you are buying a security that is new to your portfolio, Quicken will walk you through a quick Wizard to add the new security.

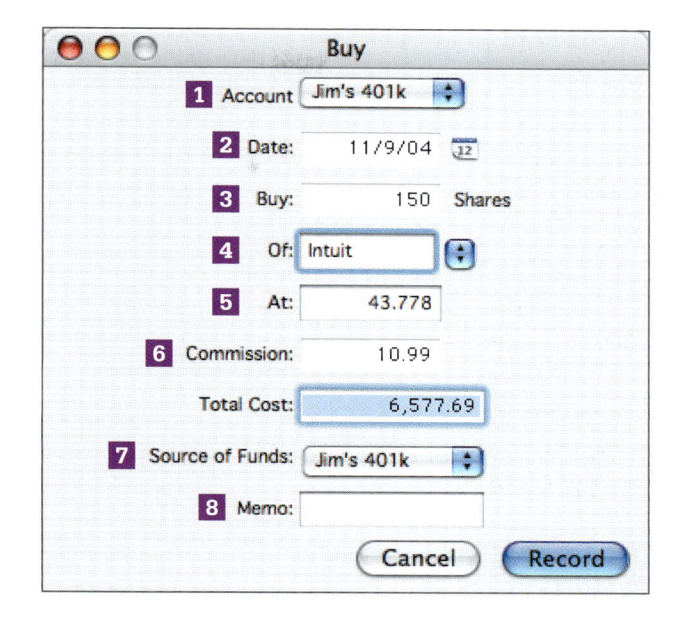

5 Enter the share price in the *At* field.

6 Enter the *Commission* amount. Quicken calculates the *Total Cost*.

7 Use the *Source of Funds* pop-up menu to specify where the money for the purchase is coming from.

8 If you like, add a *Memo*.

9 Click Record to save your transaction.

manage investments

deal with dividends

There are many transactions that can occur in your investment accounts that are not the result of buying or selling shares of securities with cash. The most common are dividends in a portfolio account and capital gains distributions and reinvestments in single mutual fund accounts.

To enter these transactions manually, you will use the investment action forms again. On Windows, select the investment account in the Account Bar, click the Transactions tab, then click Enter Transactions. In the investment actions dialog, choose the kind of transaction you need to enter, then fill out the dialog.

On the Mac, choose Activities > Investment Actions. The Investment Actions window appears. Double-click the investment action you want, and the associated action form appears. Fill out the form, and click Record.

If your financial institution supports it, downloading investment transactions gives you many of the same benefits as online banking, namely less manual entry, better accuracy, and a significant time savings.

To download investment transactions on Windows, click the One Step Update button in the toolbar, then choose the accounts that you want to update in the One Step Update dialog, then click Update Now. Quicken will go online, connect to your financial institutions, and download any transactions that are available.

Accounts that have downloaded investment transactions that need to be reviewed will be flagged in the Account Bar.

Flag —— Ameritrade IRA   9,638.55

Click the flag to open the account and review your transaction. On the Transactions tab of the account, the bottom half of the window will show the downloaded transactions. Click to select a transaction, and Accept and Delete buttons will appear below the transaction. If the transaction is OK, click Accept. The transaction will appear in the transaction list.

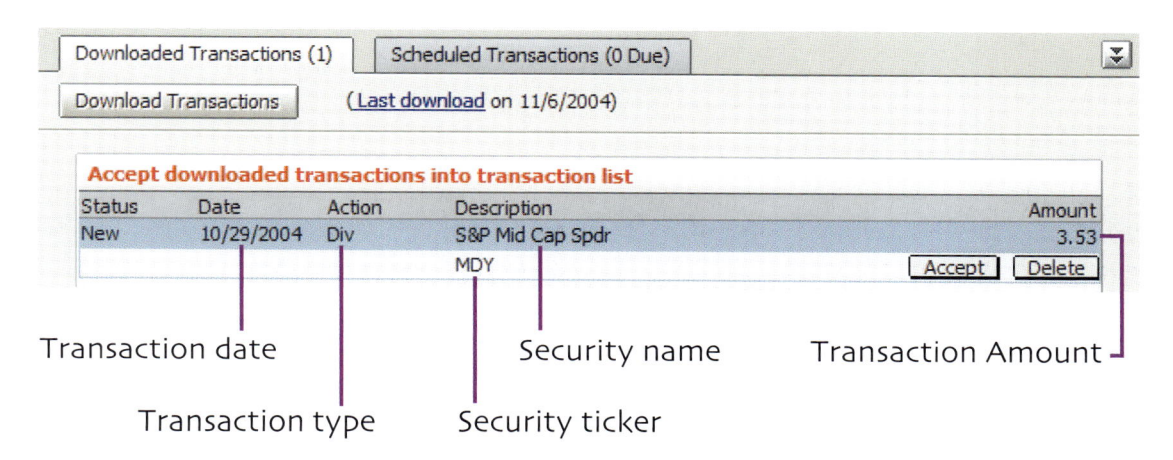

Status	Date	Action	Description	Amount
New	10/29/2004	Div	S&P Mid Cap Spdr	3.53
			MDY	

Transaction date — Transaction type — Security name — Security ticker — Transaction Amount

On the Mac, begin downloading investment transactions by clicking the Download button in the Investing section of the toolbar. The Download Transactions window appears. Choose the investment account you want from the pop-up menu at the top the window, then click the Get Online Data button. Quicken goes online and downloads the transactions, which are displayed in the Download Transactions window. Click the Accept button to add the downloaded items to your register.

manage investments

extra bits

add transactions (Win) p. 134

- You'll find explanations of the more exotic investment actions found in the Enter transaction pop-up menu, such as short selling, in the Quicken User Guide.

- The column at the right edge of a single mutual fund account register and a portfolio account register differs. In a portfolio account, the column shows the running Cash Balance in the account. Mutual fund accounts don't have cash balances, so the column is called Share Balance, and shows a running total of the accumulated shares in the account.

add transactions (Mac) p. 136

- When you're selling a security, if you leave the Destination of Funds field blank, Quicken credits the proceeds of the sale to the Portfolio account, which increases the cash balance in the account. This doesn't work for single mutual fund accounts, because such accounts can't have a cash balance.

- The number of investment transactions available in a mutual fund account is smaller than the transactions available in a portfolio account, because a portfolio account provides a wider array of investment options. For example, you can short sell a security in a portfolio account, but you can't short sell a mutual fund.

deal with dividends p. 138

- Unlike online banking, online investment transactions through Quicken are a one-way trip; you can enter transactions in Quicken by downloading them, but you can't use Quicken to create new transactions, such as buying or selling securities. For that, you'll need to use your online broker's Web site, or even talk to your broker on the telephone.

- You enable an investment account for online transactions in the same way that you online enable any other account. If you need help, see Chapter 5.

index

401(k) investments, 122
403(k) investments, 122
[] (brackets), 38, 95

A

accepting transactions, 69–70
account balance
    adjusting, 90
    location of, 8
Account Bar (Windows Home page), 5
Account List, 10, 11, 22
account registers. See registers
accounting mistakes, 89–90, 91
accounts. See also checking accounts; credit card accounts
    asset and liability, 96
    balancing, 85–91
    Cash, 28–29
    enabling online, 62–65
    flagged, 138
    home mortgage
        Mac, 99–101
        Windows, 96–98
    portfolio
        Cash Balance column, 140
        choosing detail to enter, 120
        Mac, 125–126, 132
        Windows, 121–124, 132
    setting up, 19–24
        Mac, 22–23
        tips for, 28–29
        Windows, 19–21
activity area tabs (Mac), 9
activity centers (Windows), 6
Add 401(k) Deduction dialog (Windows), 34
Add a PIN dialog (Windows), 73
Add Pre-Tax Deduction button, 34
Add Vault Password dialog (Windows), 73
Adjust Balance dialog, 90
asset accounts, 96
assets, 17

Assign tax link checkbox (Mac Set Up Category dialog), 27
ATM transactions, 83
Auto-Reconcile, 83, 91

B

backups, 15
balancing accounts, 85–91
    adjusting account balance, 90
    comparing bank statement with transactions, 87
    correcting differences, 88, 89–90, 91
    entering data from statement, 20, 86
    overview, 85
bank accounts. See checking accounts
bank statements, 20, 86, 87
banks. See financial institutions
Bills and Scheduled Transactions list (Windows Home screen), 5
bonds. See securities
brackets ([]), 38, 95
broker commission, 135, 137
brokers. See online brokerage access
buttons
    Add Pre-Tax Deduction, 34
    Checks, 54
    custom account, 9
    Don't show me this again, 118
    on Mac toolbars, 13, 14
    Open Split, 11, 42
    Portfolio, 136
    Registers, 136
    Transfer, 52
    Write Checks, 54
Buy dialog (Mac), 137
buying securities, 134–139

C

calculator, 57–58
calendar
    displaying
        Mac, 37

index

Windows, 33
scheduling mortgage payments, 106
canceling split transactions, 58
capital gains distributions, 138–139
car loans. See loans
Cash account, 28–29
Cash Flow Center (Windows), 17, 19
categories
    adding to split transactions, 58
    custom report, 111
    QuickFill feature, 40
    setting up
        Mac, 4, 8, 27
        Windows, 25–26
    transfer, 24, 38, 95
    using, 24, 29
Categories & Transfers dialog (Mac), 27
Category List dialog (Windows), 25
check. See paychecks
checking accounts. See also online banking
    adding
        Mac, 22–23
        Windows, 19–20
    downloading transactions from, 66–67
Checks button (Mac), 54
Clr column, 87, 88
comparing transactions, 68–73
    EFTs, 83
    Macs, 71–72
    reconciling account after, 83
    Windows, 68–70
Configure Toolbar dialog, 14, 16
cost basis, 120, 124
Create PIN Vault dialog (Mac), 74
Create Quicken File dialog (Windows), 2
Create Scheduled Transaction dialog (Windows), 48–51
credit card accounts
    downloading transactions, 105
    entering charges to, 94, 105
    late fees, 105
    making payments, 95
    overview, 93
    scheduling payments, 105
    setting up
        Mac, 23
        Windows, 21
custom account buttons, 9
custom reports, 113–114, 118
Customize Tool Bar dialog, 12
Customize window, 111–112

customizing
    reports, 111–114, 118
    toolbars, 12, 14

D

data entry
    eliminating errors, 91
    entering
        card charges, 94, 105
        statement balances, 86
    QuickFill, 40, 57
    QuickMath, 57
data files
    accounts within, 17
    backing up, 15
    creating, 2–4
    naming Windows, 2
    security for online, 82–83
date field shortcuts, 44
dates
    quick entry of, 44, 57
    report, 108–109, 110
debt. See loans
deleting
    categories, 29
    transactions, 47
deposits
    amount of, 8
    entering, 43–44, 57–58
    split transactions for, 31
Did Check(s) Print OK? dialog, 56
Direct Connect, 66, 82
dividends, 138–139, 140
Download Transactions window (Mac), 71, 72
downloading transactions
    comparing transactions, 68–73
    credit card, 105
    eliminating errors by, 91
    from financial institutions, 66–67, 91, 120
    investment dividends, 138–139
    securities quotes, 131, 132
    steps for, 66–67

E

Earnings section (Set Up Paycheck dialog), 33
EasyAnswer reports, 108–109
Edit Loan dialog (Windows), 97
Edit Loan Payment dialog (Windows), 98
Edit Tax Item dialog (Windows), 35

editing transactions, 47
EFTs (Electronic Funds Transfer), 83, 84
enabling
    Auto-Reconcile, 91
    online banking, 62–65
Enter New PIN dialog (Windows), 65
Enter Transaction dialog (Mac), 36–39
    entering
        categories and subcategories, 40
        split transactions, 37
    scheduling transactions, 36, 39
entering transactions, 43–44, 57–58
ESPP (Employee Stock Purchase Plan), 35, 38
estimating transaction amounts, 49
expense categories, 24
expense graph (Mac Insights page), 11

F

fees
    late, 105
    transfer, 84
fields, 42
financial analysis
    EasyAnswer reports, 108–109
    viewing
        deductible expenses, 107
        investment performance, 127–128
        year-to-date comparisons, 118
financial information, 17–29
    deciding what to manage, 18, 28
    setting up accounts, 19–24
        Mac, 22–23
        tips for, 28–29
        Windows, 19–21
financial institutions
    downloading
        investment dividends, 138–139
        transactions from, 66–67, 91, 120
    online banking with, 62–65, 82–83
    online brokerage access for Macs, 125, 132
    setting Windows portfolio accounts for, 121–124

G

Get Started Assistant, 2
graphs
    creating, 115–116
    investment performance as, 128
    printing, 117

H

home mortgages
    making payments on, 102–103
    overview, 93
    setting up accounts
        Mac, 99–101, 106
        Windows, 96–98, 105
    tracking, 104, 106
    viewing payment schedule, 104
Home screen
    Mac version, 9–11
    toolbar, 5, 9
    Windows version, 5–7

I

iCal (Mac), 39
income categories, 24
Insights page (Mac), 11
interest rates, 97, 98, 100
Internet. See also online banking; online brokerage access
    setting up online banking, 62–65
    Web Connect, 66–67, 82
Investment Actions window (Mac), 136
Investment Transactions dialog (Windows), 133, 134
investments, 119–140
    adding transactions
        Macintosh, 136–137, 140
        Windows, 134–135, 140
    choosing detail to enter, 120
    dividends, 138–139, 140
    downloading quotes, 131, 132
    managing, 133
    overview, 119
    Portfolio window, 127–130
    setting up portfolios
        Mac, 125–126, 132
        Windows, 121–124, 132
    viewing details, 129–130
IRA accounts, 122

K

Keogh accounts, 122
keyboard shortcuts, 44

index

L

late fees, 105
liabilities, 17
liability accounts, 96, 106
Loan Interview dialog (Mac), 99
Loan Summary tab (View Loans dialog), 102
loans. See also credit card accounts
    entering card charges, 94, 105
    graphing pay offs of, 115
    making
        card payments, 95
        loan payments, 102–103
    overview, 93
    setting up mortgage accounts
        Mac, 99–101
        Windows, 96–98
    tracking mortgages, 104, 106
Loans window
    Mac, 99, 103
    Windows, 102

M

Macintosh computers
    account set up, 22–23
        credit card, 23
        mortgage, 99–101
        paycheck, 31, 36–39, 40
        portfolio, 125–126, 132
    calculator paper tape, 58
    categories, 4, 8
    Checks button, 54
    creating data files, 4
    custom reports, 112
    Home screen, 9–11
    mortgage payments
        making, 103
        scheduling, 101, 106
    One Step Update, 76
    organizing PINs, 74
    Portfolio window, 128, 130
    registers for, 42
    selecting, 4
    starting Quicken, 1
    toolbar
        buttons on, 13, 14
        customizing, 14
        Home screen, 9
    transactions
        comparing, 71–72
        entering, 43–44

investment, 136–137, 140
    scheduling, 50–51
    transferring money, 53
    viewing investments, 130
Make Regular Payment dialog (Windows), 103
managing investments. See investments
matched transactions, 68, 71
Memorize Report Template dialog (Mac), 114
memorized reports, 113, 114
menu bar, 5, 9
mistakes, 89–90, 91
mortgages. See home mortgages
mutual funds. See also securities
    capital gains distributions, 138–139
    price updates for, 132
    Share Balance columns for Windows, 140
    specifying, 122

N

naming categories, 29
net worth statement, 29
New Account Assistant window (Mac), 22–23, 125
numbers
    data entry shortcuts, 44
    negative, 38

O

One Step Update
    downloading quotes with, 131, 132
    online banking with, 75–76
    sending online payments with, 79
Online Account Setup dialog, 62, 63
Online Account Updates window (Mac), 74, 76
online banking
    about, 61
    Auto-Reconcile, 83, 91
    bill payment
        about, 51
        creating online payees, 77–78
        paying bills online, 79
        scheduling EFTs, 84
    changing PIN for, 65
    comparing downloaded transactions, 68–73, 83
    downloading
        checking transactions, 66–67
        credit card transactions, 105
    eliminating data entry errors, 91
    One Step Update for, 75–76
    organizing PINs
        Mac, 74, 83

Windows, 73, 83
setting up, 62–65, 82–83
transferring money online, 80–81
online brokerage access
online investing, 140
setting up
Mac, 125, 132
Windows, 121–124, 132
Online Center dialog (Windows), 80
Online Payees List dialog (Windows), 77
Open Split button (Mac), 11, 42

P

passwords, 73, 83
Paycheck Setup assistant (Windows), 32
paychecks, 31–59
account registers, 42
editing transactions, 47
entering transactions, 43–44, 57–58
numbering written and printed, 59
numbers on transaction line, 8
postdated, 57
printing, 56, 59
scheduling transactions, 48–51
setting up
Mac, 31, 36–39, 40
Windows, 31, 32–35, 40
setting up to print, 54
splitting transactions, 31, 45–46, 58
transferring money, 52–53
Mac, 53
Windows, 52–53
writing, 54–55, 59
payees, 8, 77–78
Payees dialog (Mac), 77
Payment dialog (Mac), 103
payments. See also online banking
making credit card, 95
mortgage
Mac, 99–104, 106
Windows, 96–98, 102–104, 105
online, 79
payment amount, 8
scheduling EFTs, 84
personal data screen (Windows), 3
PIN (personal identification number)
changing, 65
organizing
Mac, 74, 83
Windows, 73, 83
using, 62, 63

PIN Vault Setup dialog (Windows), 73
placeholder transactions, 122
portfolio accounts
Cash Balance column for Windows, 140
choosing detail to enter, 120
setting up
Mac, 125–126, 132
Windows, 121–124, 132
Portfolio button (Mac), 136
Portfolio window, 127–130
portfolios, 110
postdated checks, 57
preprinted checks, 54, 59
pre-tax deductions, 34–35, 36
Preview Payment dialog (Mac), 101
principal and interest
Mac, 100
tracking, 96
viewing, 106
Windows, 98
Print Checks dialog (Mac), 56
Print dialog (Windows), 117
printing
paychecks, 56, 59
PIN Vault listing, 83
reports and graphs, 117

Q

Quicken
creating data files, 2–4
starting, 1
what data to manage, 18, 28
Quicken Account Setup assistant (Windows), 96, 105
QuickFill, 40, 57
QuickMath, 57
QuickZoom, 118

R

Reconcile Online Account dialog (Windows), 91
Reconcile Startup dialog (Mac), 86
reconciliation
adjusting account balance, 90
after comparing transactions, 83
Auto-Reconcile, 83, 91
entering data from statement, 86
finding mistakes in, 88, 89–90, 91
Reconciliation Complete dialog (Windows), 88
reconciliation reports, 88

index

Register (Enter Transaction dialog), 36
registers
    comparing downloaded transactions with, 68–72
    Mac, 10
    Portfolio account, 126
    sorting options for, 57
    Transfer button on Windows, 52
    transferring money between, 52–53
    using, 42
    Windows, 7
Registers button (Mac), 136
reinvestments, 138–139
reminders, 51
reports, 107–118
    building custom, 111–112
    EasyAnswer, 108–109
    overview, 107
    printing, 117
    reconciliation, 88
    saving custom, 113–114, 118
    standard, 110, 118
Reports and Graphs window (Windows), 108
Reports window (Mac), 109
Review Accounts dialog, 65

S

Save dialog (Mac), 4
Save Report dialog (Windows), 113
saving
    custom reports, 113–114, 118
    Quicken data, 3, 4
Schedule Future Transaction dialog (Mac), 50
scheduling
    paychecks, 36, 40
    payments
        credit card, 105
        EFT, 84
        mortgage (Mac), 101, 106
    transactions, 48–51
Scheduling area
    Create Scheduled Transaction dialog, 48, 49
    Enter Transaction dialog, 36
    Schedule Future Transaction dialog, 50, 51
    Set Up Paycheck dialog, 33
securities
    buying, 134–139
    cost basis for, 124
    defined, 110
    dividends, 138–139, 140
    downloading quotes, 131, 132
    ticker symbols, 123, 126
    viewing
        details, 129–130
        performance, 127–128
security, online, 82–83
Select Checks to Print dialog (Windows), 56
service charges, 83, 91
Set Up Category dialog, 25, 26, 27
Set Up Loan dialog (Mac), 100
Set Up Online Payee dialog, 78
Set Up Paycheck dialog (Windows)
    deductions, 34–35
    Earnings section, 33
    entering net pay only, 40
    illustrated, 31
    Scheduling area, 33
    varying paycheck amounts, 40
setting up accounts
    Mac, 22–23
        credit cards, 23
        mortgages, 99–101, 106
        paychecks, 31, 36–39, 40
    online banking, 62–65, 82–83
    tips for, 28–29
    Windows, 19–21
        credit cards, 21
        mortgages, 96–98, 105
        paychecks, 31, 32–35, 40
sorting registers, 57
Split Transaction dialog, 45, 46
split transactions
    canceling, 58
    entering, 45–46
        Mac, 37
        Windows, 31
    illustrated, 11, 37
    loan payments as, 106
standard reports, 110, 118
starting Quicken, 1
Statement Summary dialog (Windows), 86–87
stocks. See securities
subcategories, 24, 29, 40

T

taxes
    assigning tax links, 27
    pre-tax deductions, 34–35, 36
    viewing deductible expenses, 107
Tax-related checkbox (Mac Set Up Category
    dialog), 27

ticker symbols, 123, 126
toolbars
   customizing, 12, 14
   Home screen, 5, 9
   Mac buttons on, 13, 14
   Windows buttons, 12
transaction line (Windows Home screen), 8
transactions
   accepting downloaded, 69–70
   adding to iCal, 39
   categories of, 8
   comparing downloaded, 68–73
   downloading
      credit card, 105
      eliminating errors by, 91
      from financial institutions, 66–67, 91, 120
      investment dividends, 138–139
      securities quotes, 131, 132
      steps for, 66–67
      Web Connect, 66–67, 82
   editing, 47
   entering, 43–44, 57–58
   finding mistakes in, 89–90
   investment
      adding Mac, 136–137, 140
      adding Windows, 134–135, 140
      entering Windows, 121–124
   new downloaded, 70–72
   scheduling, 39, 48–51
   split
      canceling, 58
      entering, 31, 37, 45–46
      illustrated, 11, 37
   voiding, 47
Transfer button (Windows), 52
transfer categories
   brackets around, 38, 95
   defined, 24
   using, 38
Transfer dialog (Windows), 53
Transfer Money Between Quicken Registers dialog (Mac), 53
Transfer Money Online dialog (Mac), 81
transferring money
   between registers
      Macs, 53
      Windows, 52–53
   online, 80–81
      about, 61
      fees for, 84
      scheduling payments, 84
   transfer categories, 24, 38

U

user interface, 1

V

versions of Quicken, 1
View Loans dialog (Windows), 102–103
viewing
   deductible expenses, 107
   investment details, 129–130
   investments, 127–128
   mortgage payment schedule, 104
   principal and interest, 106
voiding transactions, 47

W

Web Connect, 66–67, 82
Windows computers
   account set up, 19–21
      credit card, 21
      mortgage, 96–98
      paychecks, 31, 32–35, 40
      portfolio, 121–124, 132
   backing up data files, 15
   calculator, 57
   comparing downloaded transactions, 68–70
   creating data files, 2–3, 4
   customizing, reports, 111
   entering transactions, 43–44
   Home screen, 5–7
   investment transactions, 134–135, 140
   mortgage payments, 102–103
   One Step Update, 75–76
   organizing PINs, 73
   Portfolio window, 127–129
   registers, 7, 42
   starting Quicken, 1
   toolbar
      customizing, 12
      Home screen, 5
   transferring money, 52–53
   versions of Quicken, 1
   viewing investments, 129
   Write Checks button, 54
Write Checks window (Mac), 10, 55
writing paychecks, 54–55, 59

Y

year-to-date comparisons, 118

Safari® BOOKS ONLINE ENABLED

THIS BOOK IS SAFARI ENABLED

INCLUDES FREE 45-DAY ACCESS TO THE ONLINE EDITION

The Safari® Enabled icon on the cover of your favorite technology book means the book is available through Safari Bookshelf. When you buy this book, you get free access to the online edition for 45 days.

Safari Bookshelf is an electronic reference library that lets you easily search thousands of technical books, find code samples, download chapters, and access technical information whenever and wherever you need it.

TO GAIN 45-DAY SAFARI ENABLED ACCESS TO THIS BOOK:

- Go to **http://www.peachpit.com/safarienabled**
- Complete the brief registration form
- Enter the coupon code found in the front of this book before the Table of Contents

If you have difficulty registering on Safari Bookshelf or accessing the online edition, please e-mail customer-service@safaribooksonline.com.